Table of Contents

Table of Contents

Frank Schaffer Publications®

Printed in the United States of America. All rights reserved. Limited Reproduction Permission: Permission to duplicate these materials is limited to the person for whom they are purchased. Reproduction for an entire school or school district is unlawful and strictly prohibited. Frank Schaffer Publications is an imprint of School Specialty Publishing. Copyright © 2006 School Specialty Publishing.

Send all inquiries to:
Frank Schaffer Publications
3195 Wilson Drive NW
Grand Rapids, Michigan 49534

Science—Grade 5

ISBN 0-7696-4945-9

1 2 3 4 5 6 7 8 9 10 WAL 10 09 08 07 06

Sort 'Em Out

Name _____

Vertebrates are animals with backbones. Animals without backbones are called **invertebrates**. At the bottom of the page are pictures of both kinds of animals.

Directions: Write the name of each animal under the correct heading below.

VERTEBRATES	INVERTEBRATES
1. _____	1. _____
2. _____	2. _____
3. _____	3. _____
4. _____	4. _____
5. _____	5. _____

Classifying Vertebrates

Directions: Complete the chart to show how the different classes of vertebrates are alike and how they are different.

	FISH	AMPHIBIANS	BIRDS	REPTILES	MAMMALS
Body covering					
Warm- or cold-blooded					
Lungs or gills					
Born alive or hatched					
Habitat					
Name one example					

Science: Grade 5

We can see many living things when we are on the playground. A living thing that we might see is a grasshopper. A grasshopper is a good example of an insect. It represents a typical insect with the head, thorax, and abdomen. It has three pairs of legs and two pairs of wings. The grasshopper also has two antennae, two eyes, legs, a stomach, a heart, a mouth, and breathing holes called *spiracles.*

Directions: Look at the diagram below. Use the WORD BANK to write the correct parts of the insect in the diagram and under the correct heading below. Two words are not used for the diagram.

WORD BANK

eyes	wings	heart	mouth
spiracles	stomach	legs	antennae

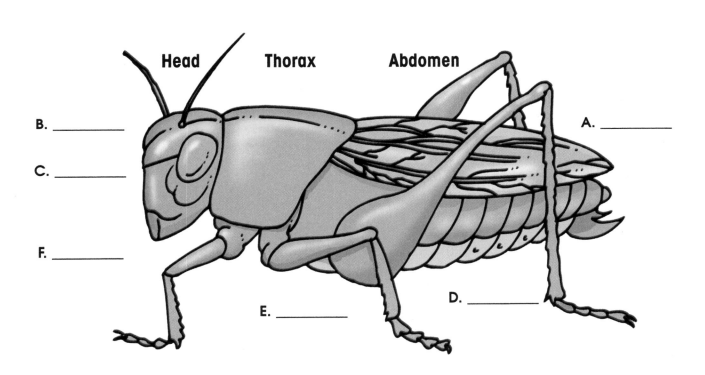

Head   **Thorax**   **Abdomen**

B. _____

C. _____

F. _____

A. _____

E. _____

D. _____

HEAD	THORAX	ABDOMEN
_____	_____	_____
_____	_____	_____
_____	_____	_____

Name _____

A reptile is an animal that has dry, scaly skin and breathes using lungs. It is a vertebrate.

Directions: Complete the word grid by filling in the squares with the names of the reptiles below.

WORD BANK

adder	caiman	gavial	leopard frog	python
alligator	cobra	gecko	lizard	spring pepper
anole	corn snake	green toad	mamba	tuatara
boa	crocodile	iguana	newt	turtle
viper				

A L L K I N D S O F R E P T I L E S

Name

Seashells are a lot of fun to collect and examine. What once lived in these shells?

Directions: Learn the names of some shells by completing the word grid below.

WORD BANK

clam	cowrie	moon	periwinkle	triton
conch	jingle	murex	scallop	tulip
cone	limpet	nerite	scotch bonnet	wentletrap
coquina	margin	olive	slipper	whelk

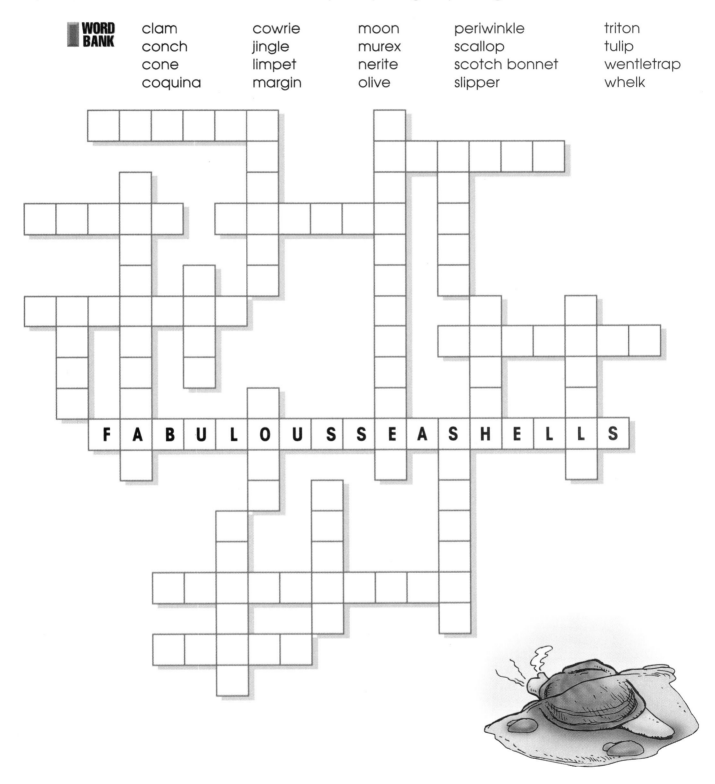

F A B U L O U S S E A S H E L L S

Name

Animals adapt so they can survive in certain conditions. One special way that some animals have adapted is **camouflage**. Using camouflage helps many animals survive in their environment. They are not readily visible to their predators.

Directions:

1. Think of an animal that relies on camouflage to help it survive. Draw the animal below.

2. Explain how the camouflage specifically helps the animal.

_____

_____

3. List important things to consider about camouflage.

a._____

b._____

c._____

Your Body Parts

Directions: Use the words from the WORD BANK to label all these parts of your body.

WORD BANK

forehead	nose	cheek	hip
chest	forearm	palm	instep
abdomen	thumb	thigh	sole
calf	heel	shoulder	shin

Name _____

Directions: Use the WORD BANK to complete the puzzle.

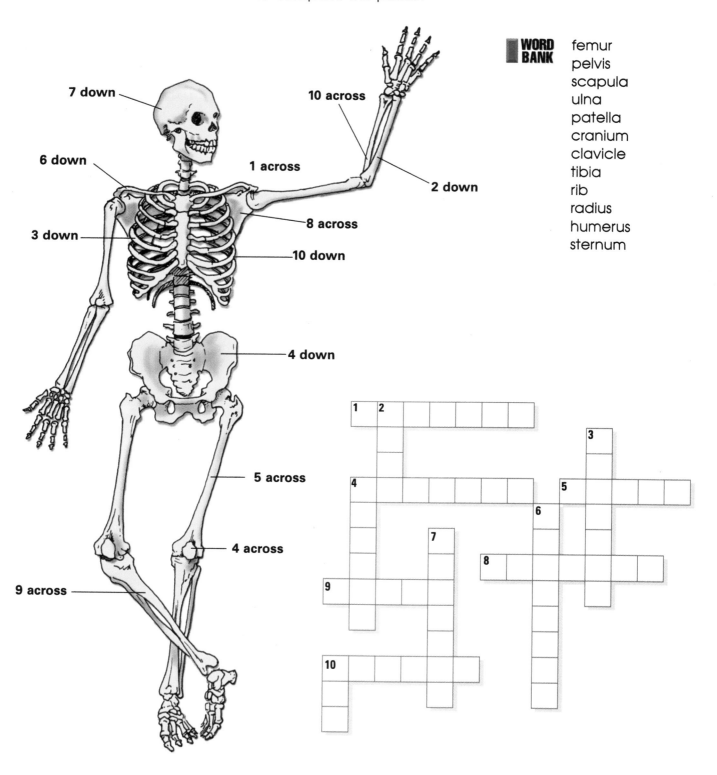

7 down
6 down
3 down
10 across
1 across
2 down
8 across
10 down
4 down
5 across
4 across
9 across

WORD BANK
femur
pelvis
scapula
ulna
patella
cranium
clavicle
tibia
rib
radius
humerus
sternum

Muscle Man

There are hundred of muscle groups in your body.

Directions: Label these muscles that appear on the surface of your body.

Common Name (*Scientific Name*)

chest muscles (*pectorals*)   thigh muscles (*quadraceps*)
calf muscles (*gastrocnemius*)   shoulder muscles (*deltoids*)
head muscles (*sternocleidomastoids*) stomach muscles (*inter coastals*)
biceps   triceps

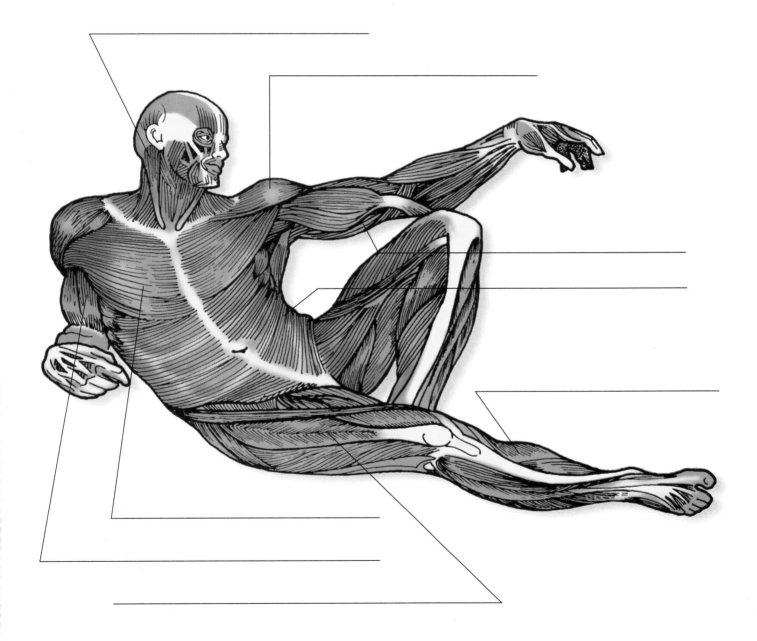

Name _____

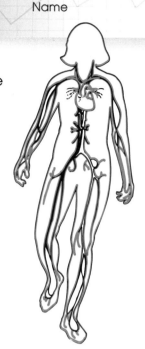

Directions: Read the information below. Underline the two main functions and the main organ of the circulatory system. Then, answer the questions. The **circulatory system** is responsible for transporting materials throughout the body and for regulating body temperature. The heart is vital to the circulatory system. It pumps blood to all parts of the body. The blood then carries nutrients and other important materials to the cells. Blood also carries waste products away from cells to disposal sites like the liver, lungs, and kidneys.

The circulatory system also acts as a temperature control for the body. Warmer blood from the center of the body is brought to the surface to be cooled. On a cold day, the blood vessels contract very little allowing little blood to flow through. This is why skin might appear pale, or even blue. However, in hot weather, blood vessels widen and more blood is able to flow through them to increase the loss of heat. Thus, your skin looks pinker and feels warmer.

1. What are the two main functions of the circulatory system? _____

   _____

2. The blood carries important nutrients to the _____

3. Blood carries _____ away from cells and to the _____,

   _____, and _____.

4. Warmer blood is brought from the _____ of the body to

   the _____ of the body to be cooled.

5. In cold weather, why does your skin appear pale, or even blue? _____

   _____

A "HEARTY" EXPERIMENT

You will need: a tennis ball and a watch with a second hand.

Hold the tennis ball in your stronger hand and give it a hard squeeze. This is about the strength it takes your heart muscle to contract to pump one beat. Squeeze the ball as hard as you can and release it 70 times in 1 minute.

Record how your hand feels. _____

Conclusion: _____

_____

Name

There are two circulatory systems in the human body. Each begins and ends in the heart. The larger system is called the **systemic circulatory system**. It branches out to all parts of the body with oxygenated blood and returns to the heart with "bad blood." The smaller system is called the **pulmonary circulatory system**. It is much shorter because it travels only to the lungs and back to the heart with oxygenated blood.

Blood vessels that carry blood to the heart are called **veins**. Those that carry it away are called **arteries**. Blood from the systemic circulatory system flows from the **superior** and **interior vena cavas** into the **right atrium**, then into the **right ventricle** and out through the **pulmonary arteries** to the lungs. At the same time, blood from the lungs enters the atrium from pulmonary veins, drops into the **left ventricle**, is pumped into the body's largest artery, called the **aorta**, then flows into blood vessels that carry it to various parts of the body.

Directions:

1. Color the systemic circulatory system red.

2. Color the pulmonary circulatory system gray.

3. Draw blue arrows to show the flow of the systemic circulatory system.

4. Draw black arrows to show the flow of the pulmonary circulatory system.

5. Label the parts of the circulatory system listed in the WORD BANK. If a number in parentheses follows a part, label it that many times.

 WORD BANK

aorta
superior and inferior vena cava
right and left atriums
right and left ventricles
pulmonary veins (2)
arteries leading from aorta
pulmonary arteries (2)

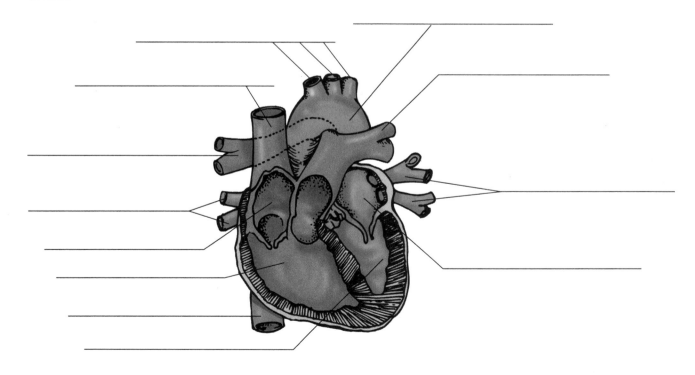

Name _____

Directions: Use the WORD BANK to complete the puzzle.

WORD BANK
lungs
heart
liver
kidneys
aorta
right atrium
right ventricle
left ventricle
left atrium
pulmonary vein
artery

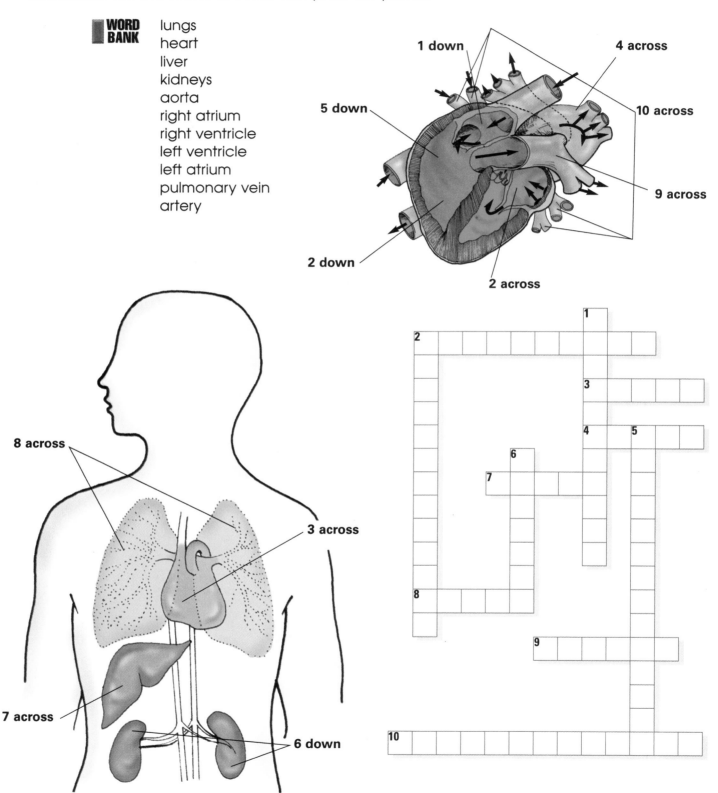

Directions: Label the parts of your **respiratory system**.

 WORD BANK

Common Name *(Scientific Name)*
throat *(pharynx)*   voice box *(larynx)*
windpipe *(trachea)*   lung cover *(pleura)*
bronchial tube   diaphragm

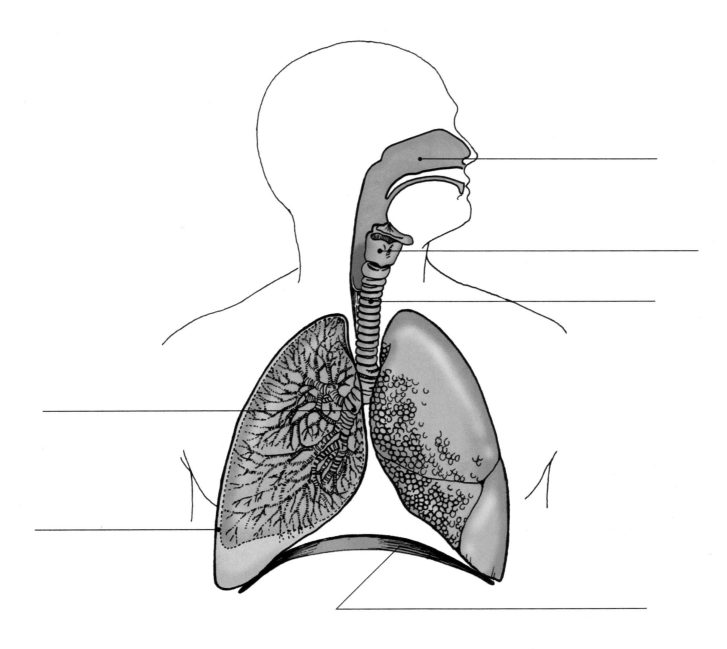

Name _____

Directions: Use the WORD BANK to complete the puzzle.

WORD BANK

diaphragm	bronchial tube	trachea	capillaries
alveoli	lung	larynx	
bronchioli	pleura	pharynx	

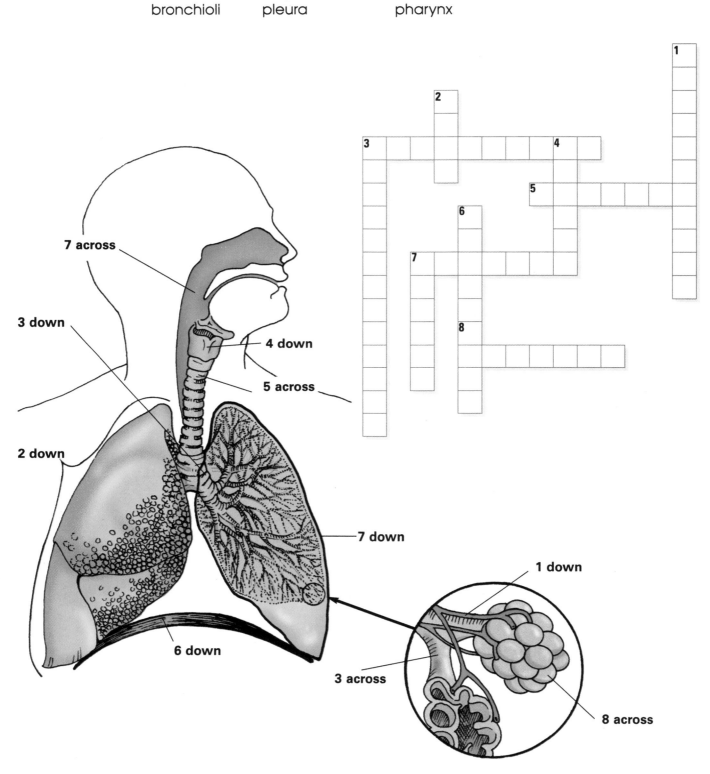

7 across

3 down

4 down

5 across

2 down

7 down

6 down

1 down

3 across

8 across

Name

Directions: Label the parts of your **digestive system**.

WORD BANK

pancreas   liver   gall bladder
stomach   mouth   large intestine
esophagus   teeth   small intestine
salivary glands   anus

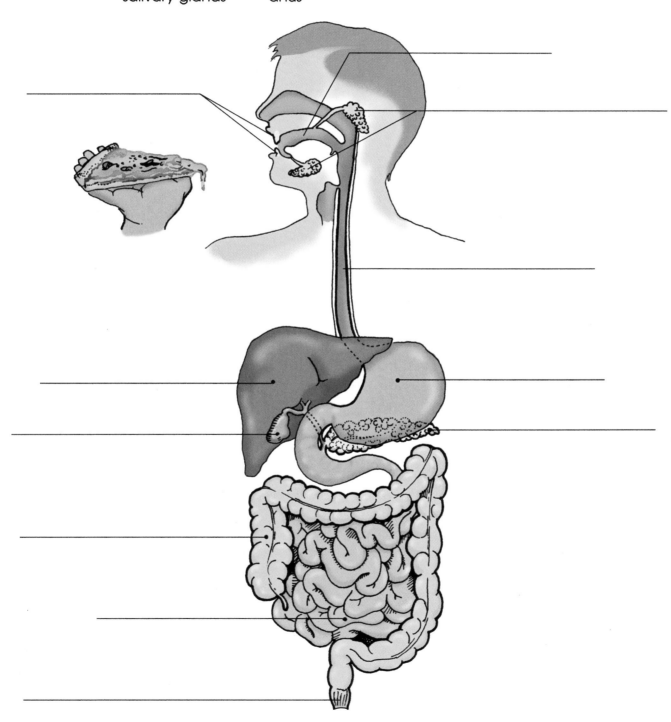

Name

The main part of the digestive system is the **alimentary canal**, a tube which starts at the mouth, and travels through the body ending at the anus.

Directions: Label the parts of the alimentary canal.

WORD BANK

anus   small intestine   esophagus
mouth   large intestine   stomach

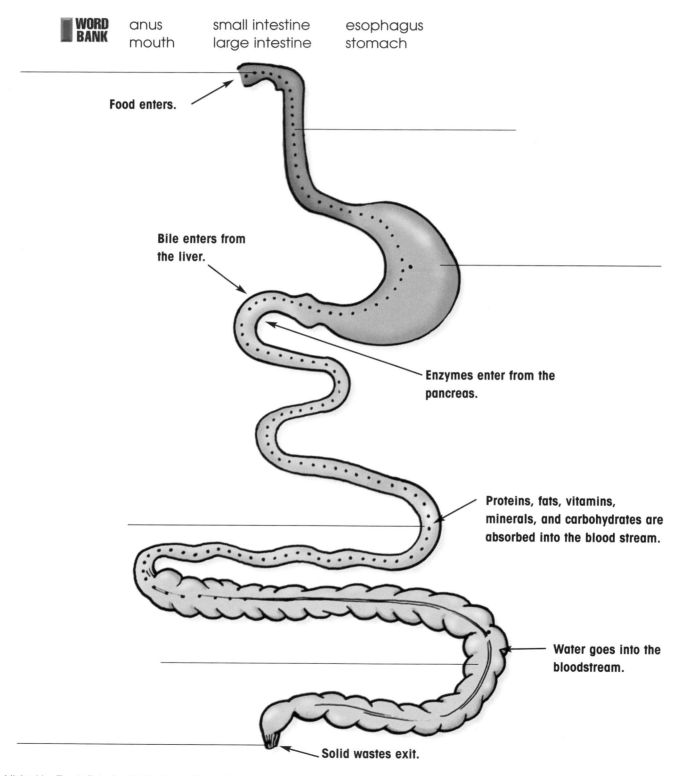

Food enters.

Bile enters from the liver.

Enzymes enter from the pancreas.

Proteins, fats, vitamins, minerals, and carbohydrates are absorbed into the blood stream.

Water goes into the bloodstream.

Solid wastes exit.

18 *Science: Grade 5*

Name

Directions: Use the WORD BANK to complete the puzzle.

WORD BANK
mouth
stomach
intestine
liver
pancreas
gall bladder
esophagus
teeth
salivary glands
anus

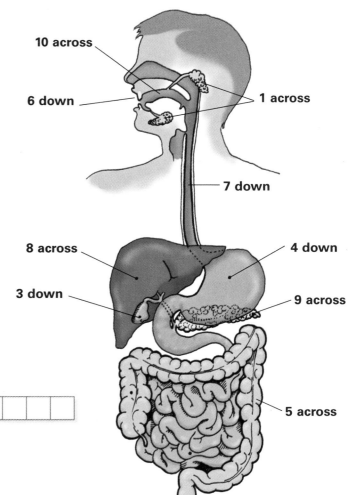

10 across

6 down

1 across

7 down

8 across

4 down

3 down

9 across

5 across

2 down

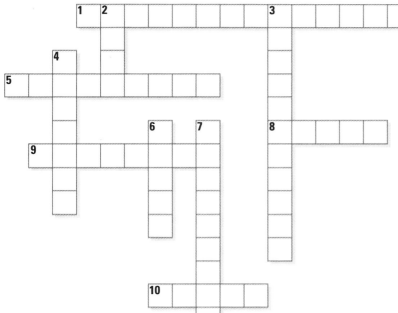

The important job of removing bodily wastes is performed by the skin and the organs of the **urinary** and **respiratory systems**.

Directions: Label the excretory organs.

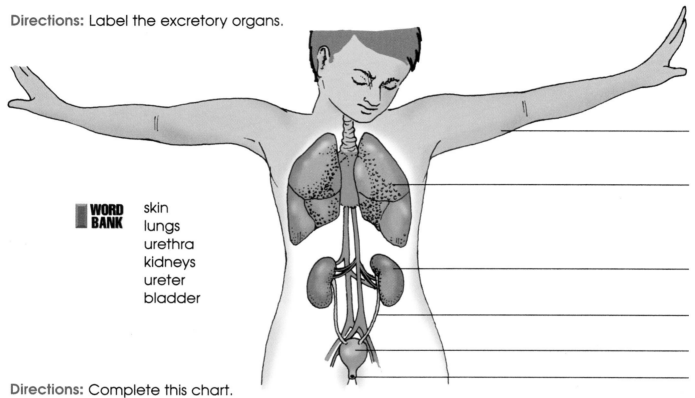

WORD BANK

skin
lungs
urethra
kidneys
ureter
bladder

Directions: Complete this chart.

FUNCTION	EXCRETORY ORGANS			
	Kidneys	**Lungs**	**Skin**	**Bladder**
Removes water				
Brings oxygen to blood				
Removes salt				
Stores urine				
Removes carbon dioxide				
Produces urine				
Removes body heat				

Name _____

Directions: Label the different parts of your body's **urinary system**.

WORD BANK

vein   artery   ureter
kidney   bladder   urethra
muscle

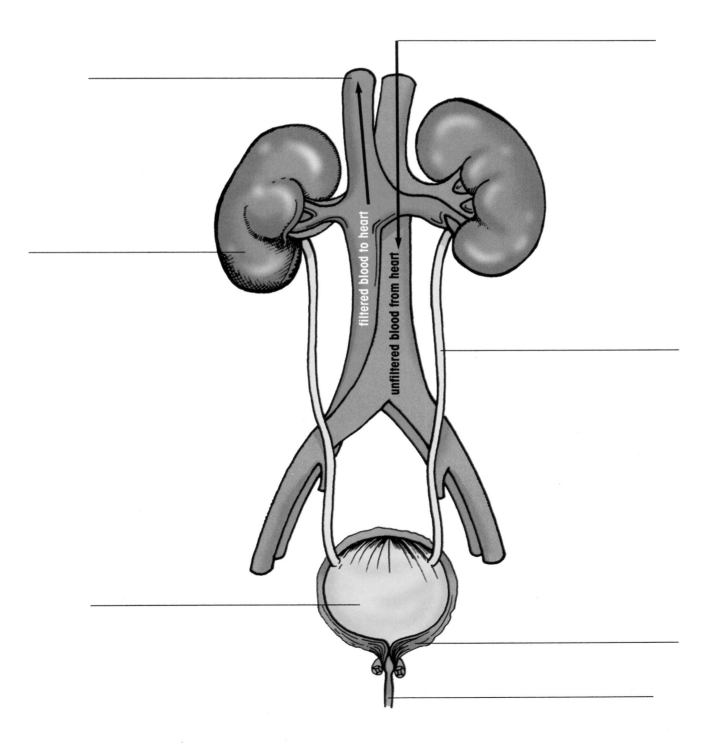

Name _____

Your body's **central nervous system** is made up of two parts: the **brain** and the **spinal cord**. The rest of the system consists of nerves coming from the brain and the spinal cord. These nerves are called **sensory nerve cells** and **motor nerve cells**. A stimulus causes your sensory nerve cells to carry messages from your skin and sense organs to your brain.

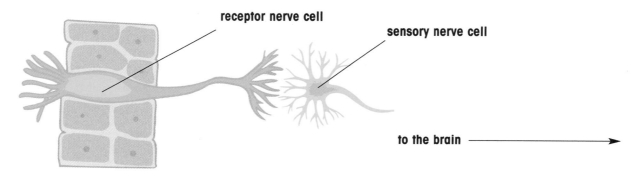

receptor nerve cell

sensory nerve cell

to the brain ⟶

Imagine you see a bee coming to sting you. Your sensory nerve cells carry this message to your brain. Your brain is the control center that interprets the message. Motor nerve cells carry the message (Run!) back from the central nervous system to the muscles. Your response (running) then occurs.

Directions: Listed below are different kinds of stimuli. Write how you would respond to each stimulus in the Response column.

Example: Stimulus — Feel pain in chest **Response** — Dial 9-1-1.

STIMULI	RESPONSE
Smell of burning food	
Bad odor from outside	
Sit on sharp object	
Traffic light turns green	
Bathtub overflowing	
Dog darts in front of car	
Pitcher throws ball at you	
Gale force wind blowing	

Fascinating Fact! Did you know your nervous system contains more than 10 billion nerve cells?

Name _____

Directions: Label the parts of your **central nervous system**.

 WORD BANK

brain	spinal cord	nerves
cerebrum	cerebellum	brain stem
nerve cell		

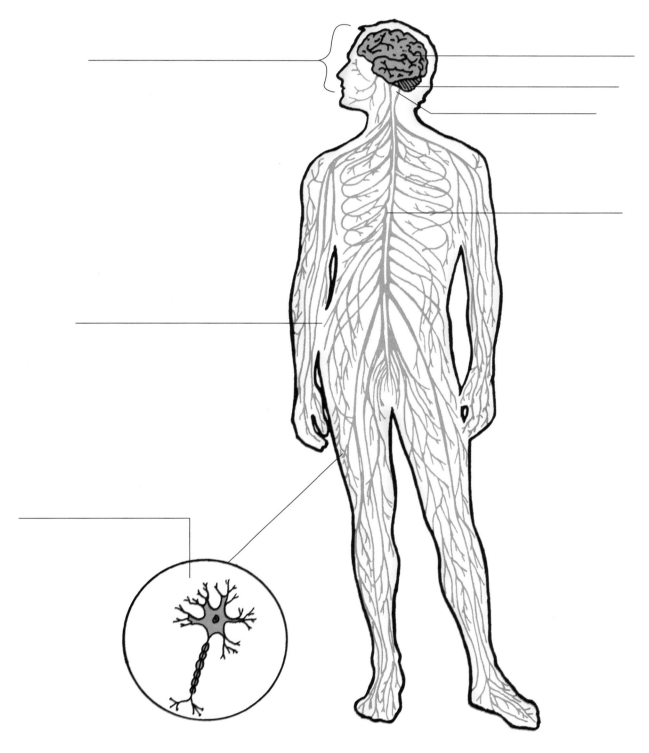

Name _____

The **endocrine glands** help control many of your body's functions.

Directions: Using the words from the WORD BANK, label the glands of the endocrine system.

WORD BANK

| thyroid gland | pituitary gland | pineal gland | pancreas |
| adrenal glands | ovaries (female) | testes (male) | |

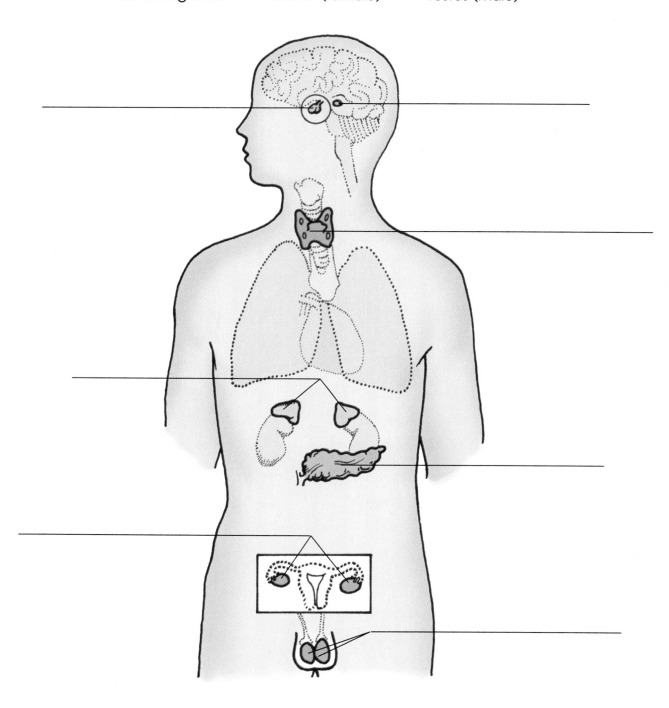

Skin Deep

Your skin is made up of many layers. These layers contain hairs, nerves, blood vessels, and glands.

Directions: Label these layers and other parts using the words from the WORD BANK.

WORD BANK

epidermis	dermis	fat layer	hair muscle
fat cells	hair	oil gland	blood vessel
sweat gland	pore	nerve	

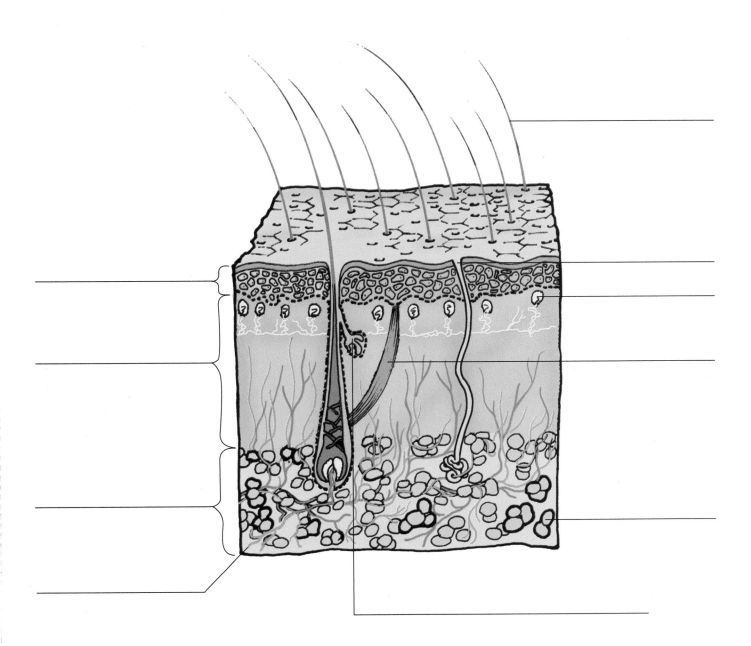

Body Tissues

Many of the body's organs are made of a variety of tissues working together. There are four kinds of tissue: **connective**, **epithelial**, **muscle**, and **nerve**. Each has a specialized function.

Directions: Study the pictures and read the descriptions. Write the name of each tissue beneath its description. Then, label the tissue parts in each picture.

 WORD BANK

connective tissue	epithelial tissue	muscle tissue
nerve tissue	collagen	fibroblast
nerve fiber	cell nucleus	cell

Composed of relatively few cells and surrounded by larger amounts of nonliving material. Supports and connects other tissues.

_____

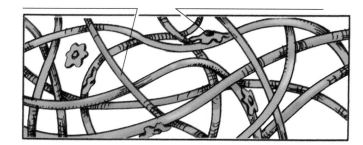

Made up of cells that can contract and relax. Allows the body to make internal and external movements.

_____

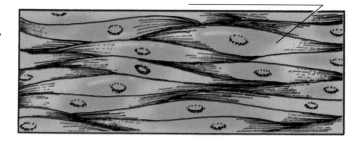

Specialized cells which carry electrical signals between the brain and other parts of the body.

_____

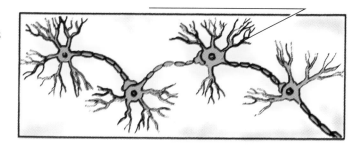

Tightly packed cells which form a covering for the skin and line the hollow internal organs.

_____

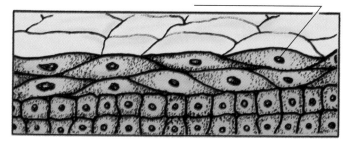

A Special Science Tool

The microscope is a necessary tool when observing tiny organisms in life science. In about 1590, two Dutch spectacle makers, Hans and Zaccharias Janssen, started experimenting with lenses. They put several lenses in a tube and made a very important discovery. The object near the end of the tube appeared to be greatly enlarged! They had just invented the compound microscope.

Other people heard of the Janssen's work and started work of their own. Galileo added a focusing device. Anthony Leeuwenhoek of Holland became so interested that he learned how to make lenses. By grinding and polishing, he was able to make small lenses with great curvatures. These rounder lenses produced greater magnification, and his microscopes were able to magnify up to 270 times.

Anthony Leeuwenhoek's new, improved microscope allowed people to see things no human had ever seen before. He saw bacteria, yeast, and blood cells. Because of his great contributions, he has been called the "Father of Microscopy."

Robert Hooke, an Englishman, also spent much of his life working with microscopes and improved their design and capabilities. He coined the word *cell* after observing cork cells under a microscope. He was reminded of a monk's cell in a monastery.

Little was done to improve the microscope until the middle of the 19th century, when great strides were made and quality instruments such as today's microscope emerged.

Directions: Use the words from the WORD BANK and a science resource book to help you label this microscope.

WORD BANK

eyepiece
fine adjustment
stage
mirror
body tube
objective
stage clips
diaphragm
coarse adjustment
arm
base
nosepiece

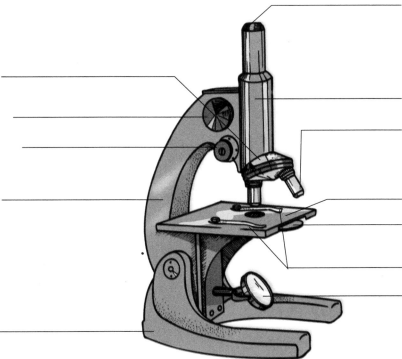

Name

Photosynthesis is a food-making process that occurs in green plants. It is the main function of the leaves.

Directions: With the help of a science book or the chart on page 149, complete the puzzle below.

ACROSS

1. Small green bodies that contain the green pigment chlorophyll
4. Gas that is released into the air as a by-product of photosynthesis
6. The escaping of water vapor from a leaf
7. Liquid obtained through the roots
8. Source of energy to power photosynthesis
9. Simple food made by photosynthesis

DOWN

2. The process by which green plants make food
3. One of the raw materials for photosynthesis is _____ dioxide.
5. Opening in the underside of a leaf

Name _____

Directions: Label the two root systems pictured below. Use the terms in the WORD BOX.

 WORD BANK   fibrous root system   root hair cell
taproot system   prop roots

Soil

_____

_____

_____

_____

29   *Science: Grade 5*

Name _____

Directions: Study the two views of a root shown below. Label the parts in both the top cross section and side cross section. Use the terms in the WORD BOX.

WORD BANK

root hairs   root cap   root tip
surface layer   branch root   food and water carrying tissues

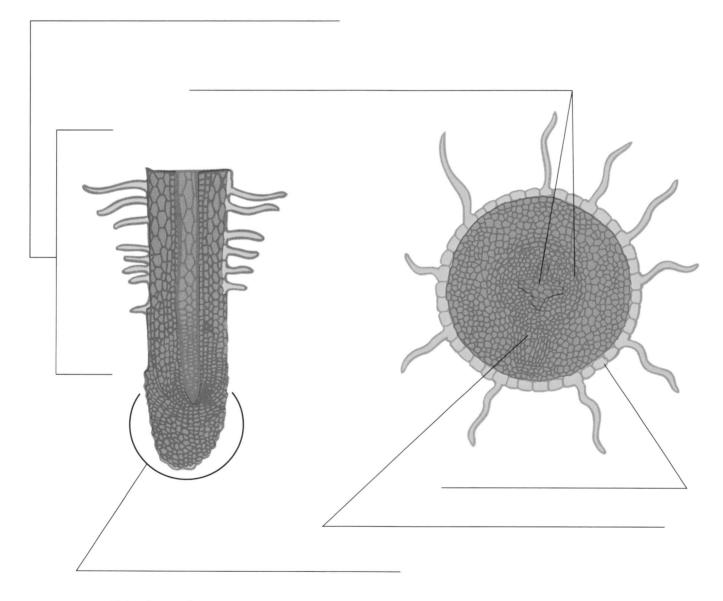

Side Cross Section

**Top Cross Section
of a Young Root**

Name _____

All of the plants you see from your porch have something in common—they all need air, warmth, water, nutrients, and time to grow. Plants continue to grow throughout their entire lives. Just like humans, plants grow from a single cell and develop into a multi-celled organism. But most plants reproduce through seeds. The seed is protected by a hard outer coating called a **seed coat**. Inside the seed is a young plant, called an **embryo**. A seed also contains food the embryo needs to stay alive. Seeds can remain inactive for months, weeks, or even years. In fact, the oldest seed ever sprouted was inactive for 1,288 years before it sprouted into a lotus plant.

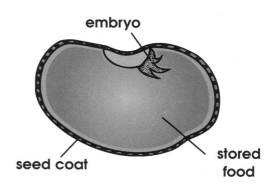

Seeds start to change in a process known as **germination**. A plant "hatches" from a seed. The seed absorbs water that causes the embryo to grow larger and "hatch" out of the seed coat as it splits open. This allows the baby plant, or embryo, to peek out and change into a sprout. The first part of the sprout to peek out is the roots. They are closely followed by the stem and leaves that push through the soil as the sprout develops into a seedling. The little seedling continues to stretch towards the sun's light that provides energy to help it grow and develop into a plant.

Directions: Use the information to answer the following questions.

1. What do all plants need? _____

_____

2. How do plants reproduce? _____

_____

3. What are the parts of a seed? _____

_____

4. What happens when a seed germinates? _____

_____

5. Which part of the embryo comes out of the seed first? _____

   Why do you think this is? _____

_____

Name _____

We know how seeds grow into plants. But how do the seeds get from one place to another? Seeds travel in many ways.

Directions: Look below at the five ways that seeds travel. Tell how each seed moves.

1.
   _____
   _____
   _____
   _____

2.
   _____
   _____
   _____
   _____

3.
   _____
   _____
   _____
   _____

4.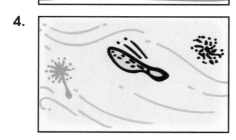
   _____
   _____
   _____
   _____

5.
   _____
   _____
   _____
   _____

Name _____

Each person in your classroom is an important part of what goes on in the classroom. Each person has a job to do, whether it is teaching, learning, or helping. Classrooms are busy and have many tools that are used to help students grow and learn.

Many plants are like that too. They have flowers that make seeds inside them. The flower has special things inside of it that help the seeds grow.

Directions: Look at the diagram and the chart below. Label and color the flower diagram using the information in the chart.

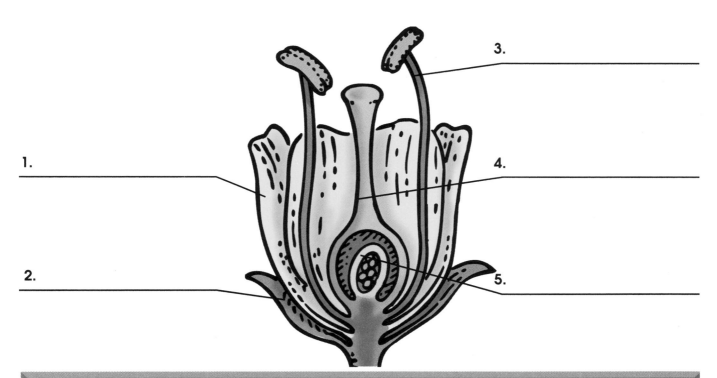

FLOWER PART	DESCRIPTION	COLOR
Pistil	A large center stalk, often shaped like a water bottle	Yellow
Stamen	Tall, thin stalk with a knobbed tip; it holds grains of pollen	Brown
Petal	Brightly colored and sweet-smelling leaves	Red
Sepal	Small, leaf-like part at the base of the flower	Green
Ovary	Ball-shaped part at the base of the pistil; this is where the seeds develop	Blue

33 *Science: Grade 5*

Name _____

Use the words from the WORD BANK to complete the puzzle. Cross out each word as you use it. The remaining words will help you answer the riddle.

WORD BANK

petals	had	chlorophyll
ache	because	flower
sun	cotyledon	leaf
tap	it	an
ear	root	sugar
photosynthesis		

ACROSS

4. Deep-growing type of root
6. Beautiful, seed-making part of the plant
7. Brightly colored "leafy" parts of the flower
9. Large part of seed that supplies food
10. Sweet food made by the leaves

DOWN

1. Making food with the help of light.
2. Green food-making material in a leaf
3. Plant's "food factory"
5. Plant's anchor
8. Plants get their energy from the _____.

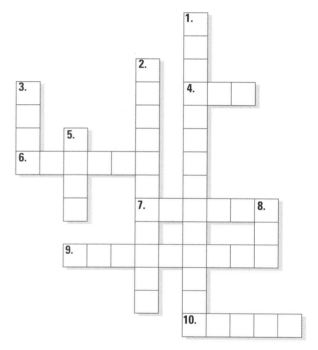

Riddle:

Why did the cornstalk go to the doctor?

_____

Name _____

Organisms are either producers or consumers, depending on the source of their energy. Consumers are either herbivores, carnivores, or omnivores.

Directions: Label the producers, omnivores, herbivores, and carnivores in each food chain.

1. a. _____ b. _____ c. _____

2. a. _____ b. _____ c. _____

3. a. _____ b. _____ c. _____

Just like plants and animals need the proper food and nutrients in their diet each day, so do people. The school lunchroom staff makes sure that the students eating there will receive a balance of the types of foods they need.

The **food pyramid** is a model that shows how many servings of certain foods students should eat each day. If students eat the proper amount of each food group they are sure to develop strong minds and bodies.

Directions: Look at the food pyramid. Write the number of each food item in the list in the correct section of the pyramid.

 WORD BANK

1. orange
2. yogurt
3. cookie
4. carrot
5. chicken leg
6. pancake

7. breakfast cereal
8. milk
9. potato
10. roast beef
11. cupcake
12. cheese

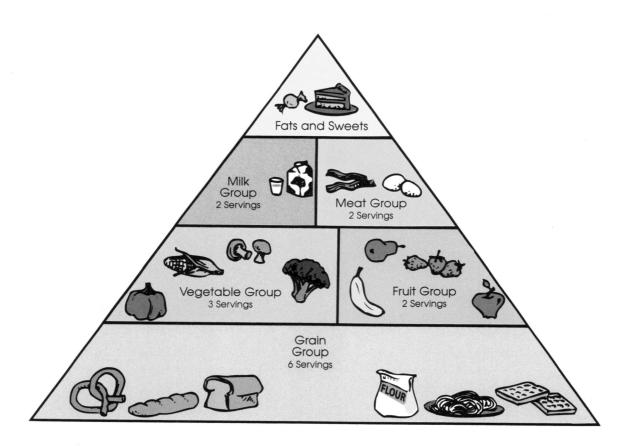

Where's the Energy?

Your garage might be full of tools. Tools need energy to work. Your body does work like the tools in your garage. This means that your body also needs energy to work. You get the energy your body needs from the foods you eat.

Foods contain nutrients that have stored energy. This stored energy is changed into fuel for your body as it is digested. The amount of energy released is measured in calories. A calorie is how much energy proteins, carbohydrates, and fats supply your body. Every gram of protein and carbohydrate provides four calories of energy. Fats provide nine calories of energy.

NUTRIENT	WHAT IT DOES	FOODS WE GET IT FROM
Proteins	Supplies energy and helps build and repair cells to form tissues for proper growth and development	Meat, fish, chicken, eggs, nuts yogurt, cheese, milk, oats, spinach, and beans
Carbohydrates	Supplies energy and helps maintain body warmth	Fruits, vegetables, bread, rice, pasta, potatoes, oatmeal, pretzels, and sugars
Fats	Serves as a source of stored energy, helps your body use vitamins, and insulates your body	Avocados, butter, meat, cheese, eggs, whole milk, nuts, and oils

The number of calories you need every day for your body to perform basic processes, such as blinking your eyes, is ten times your body weight. Most of the calories you consume should come from proteins and carbohydrates. Fats won't hurt you, but you should eat them only in moderation. The key to keeping your body healthy is to find out how many calories your body needs and to eat only as many calories as your body will use.

Directions: Use the information to answer the following questions.

1. What is a calorie? _____

2. Which nutrients supply our energy needs? _____

3. Which nutrients should you eat the most of? _____

   Why? _____

   _____

4. What happens if you consume more calories than you use?

   _____

   _____

Name _____

The labels on medicine containers give us important information. Labels should always be read carefully.

Directions: Read the information on the cough medicine labels below. Answer the questions on the lines provided.

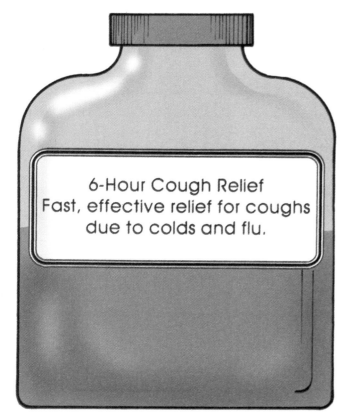

Recommended Dosage:

Children (5 - 12 years): 1 teaspoon every 6 hours.

Adults: 2 teaspoons every 6 hours.

Caution: *Do not administer to children under 5. No more than 4 dosages per day. This product may cause drowsiness; use caution if operating machinery or driving a vehicle. Should not be taken if you are pregnant or nursing a child.*

If cough or fever persists, consult a physician.

Exp. Date: 8/2006

1. What is the adult dosage? _____

2. What is a child's dosage? _____

3. What is a side effect of this medicine? _____

4. Who should not take this medicine? _____

5. How many dosages per day can be taken safely? _____

6. What is the expiration date of this medicine? _____

7. What action should be taken if the medicine does not relieve your cough?

   _____

8. For what symptoms should this medicine be taken? _____

Life on a Rotting Log

The forest community is not limited to animals and plants that live in or near living trees. As the succession of the forest continues, many trees will die and fall to the ground. The actions of plants, animals, bacteria, lichens, and weather help break the dead log down and return its components to the forest soil.

Directions: Answer the following questions.

1. List the different kinds of plant life that are found on the rotting log. _____

   _____

2. How do the small plants help the log decay? _____

   _____

3. How do the plants benefit from the log? _____

   _____

4. What kinds of small animals are found in or on the rotting log? _____

   _____

5. How do these animals help the log decay? _____

   _____

The lichen found on the rotting log is an interesting type of plant. It is actually made up of two organisms living together in symbiosis. What two organisms form a lichen? What does each of these organisms need to live? How do the organisms help each other?

_____

_____

_____

_____

Mineral Identifications

Name _____

Minerals are the most common solid materials found on the earth. Minerals may vary in the way they feel and look. Some identifying characteristics of minerals are listed below.

Directions: Use your text and reference materials to complete the mineral chart.

MINERAL	HARDNESS	SPECIFIC GRAVITY	STREAK COLOR	LUSTER
Siderite	3.5–4		white	
Gypsum		2.32		vitreous
Kaolinite			white	dull
Halite	2.5		white	
Fluorite		3–3.3		glassy
Calcite	3	2.7		
Barite		4.3–4.6	white	
Pyrite	6–6.5		green-black	
Galena		7.4–7.6		metallic
Magnetite			black	
Topaz			colorless	glassy

The hardness of a mineral is measured by its ability to be scratched. Some identification tests can be made using common items.

Hardness

0–2.5	Mineral can be scratched by one's fingernail.
3	Mineral can be scratched by a copper penny.
5.5	Mineral can be scratched with a knife but not a penny.
5.5–6.5	Mineral will scratch glass.
6.5	Mineral can be scratched slightly with a file.
above 6.5	Mineral cannot be scratched with a file.

1. Which of the minerals above can be scratched by one's fingernail? _____

_____

2. Which of the minerals above can be scratched by a copper penny?

_____

3. Which of the minerals above will scratch glass? _____

_____

4. Which of the minerals above cannot be scratched by a file? _____

_____

Published by Frank Schaffer Publications. Copyright protected. **40** Science: Grade 5

Name That Mineral

One can identify many minerals by carefully observing their physical characteristics. Some of these characteristics are:

Hardness—This is determined with a scratch test.
Color—Color depends on the substances that make up the crystals. Varies greatly.
Luster—This refers to how light reflects off the mineral.

Directions: Enough information has been given to you here to help you find the unknown minerals and fill in the chart.

MOHS HARDNESS SCALE		
HARDNESS	MINERAL	COMMON TESTS
1	Talc	Fingernail will scratch it.
2	Gypsum/Kaolinite	Fingernail will scratch it.
3	Mica/Calcite	Copper penny will scratch it.
4	Fluorite	Knife blade or window glass will scratch it.
5	Apatite/Hornblende	Knife blade or window glass will scratch it.
6	Feldspar	Will scratch a steel knife or window glass.
7	Quartz	Will scratch a steel knife or window glass.
8	Topaz	Will scratch a steel knife or window glass.
9	Corundum	Will scratch a steel knife or window glass.
10	Diamond	Will scratch all common materials.

COLOR	MINERAL
White	Quartz, Feldspar, Calcite, Kaolinite, Talc
Yellow	Quartz, Kaolinite
Black	Hornblende, Mica
Gray	Feldspar, Gypsum
Colorless	Quartz, Calcite, Gysum

LUSTER	MINERAL
Glassy	Quartz, Feldspar, Hornblende
Pearly	Mica, Gypsum, Talc
Dull	Kaolinite

The Unknown Minerals

HARDNESS	COLOR	LUSTER	MINERAL
Will scratch a steel knife or window glass.	yellow	glassy	
Will scratch a steel knife or window glass.	gray	glassy	
A copper penny will scratch it.	black	pearly	
Fingernail will scratch it.	white	pearly	
Knife blade or window glass will scratch it.	black	glassy	

41 *Science: Grade 5*

Classy Rocks

There are three main groups of rock: **igneous** rock, **metamorphic** rock, and **sedimentary** rock. Each of the rocks pictured on this page belongs to one of these groups.

Directions: Fill in the definitions. Then, in the space below each picture, tell which group each rock belongs to.

WORD BANK
layers of loose material which solidified
cooled magma
rock that has been changed into a new rock

KIND OF ROCK	DEFINITION
Igneous	
Metamorphic	
Sedimentary	

granite

gneiss

limestone

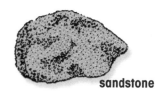
sandstone

_____

_____

_____

_____

marble

shale

basalt

_____

_____

_____

slate

obsidian

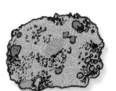
conglomerate

_____

_____

_____

Rocks and Minerals

Directions: Use what you have learned about rocks and minerals to complete this puzzle.

WORD BANK

hardness	crystal	streak
gem	cleavage	texture
fracture	luster	mineral

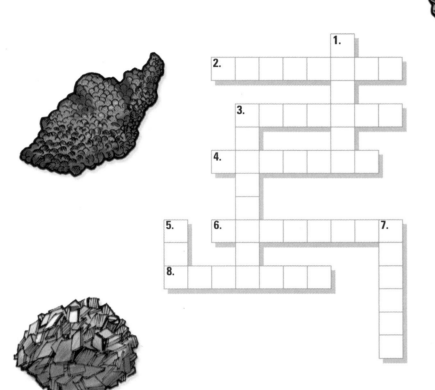

ACROSS

2. An uneven break
3. Substance with 3-dimensional plane faces
4. Feel of a surface when rubbed
6. Measured with Mohs Scale
8. Quartz is an example of a _____.

DOWN

1. Light reflected from a mineral's surface
3. Smooth break in a mineral
5. Large mineral crystal with brilliant color
7. A _____ test shows the color of a mineral when it is rubbed into a fine powder.

Glaciers

Glaciers are thick masses of ice created by the accumulation and crystallization of snow.

Directions: Match the clues about glaciers with the terms below.

1. _____ VALLEY GLACIER
2. _____ CIRQUE
3. _____ CONTINENTAL GLACIER
4. _____ CREVASSE
5. _____ DRUMLIN
6. _____ END MORAINE
7. _____ ESKER

8. _____ FIORD
9. _____ KETTLE
10. _____ PLUCKING
11. _____ ROCK FLOUR
12. _____ SURGE
13. _____ TARN
14. _____ TILL

A. Material deposited directly by a glacier

B. Glacier generally confined to mountain valleys

C. A crack in the glacier caused by movement

D. Rapid movement of a glacier

E. The process whereby a glacier loosens and lifts rocks into the ice

F. Pulverized rock caused by a glacier's abrasion

G. A bowl-shaped depression at the head of a glacial valley

H. A small lake formed after a glacier has melted away

I. A U-shaped depression formed by a glacier below sea level in a river valley that is flooded by the ocean

J. Massive accumulations of ice that cover a large portion of a landmass

K. A hilly ridge of material formed at the end of a valley glacier

L. An oval-shaped hill consisting of rock debris

M. A depression left in part of a glacier formed by the melting of a block of ice

N. Ridges of sand and gravel deposited by flowing rivers of melted ice through a glacier

Name

Do you have an apple at home? Ask an adult to cut it open. What do you see? The apple has layers. The top layer is the peel. It is thin but tough and protects the fruit. The next layer is the fruit. It can be soft or hard and most of the apple is the fruit. The inside layer is the core. It is harder than the rest of the apple and protects the seeds that are in the center.

The earth is very much like the apple. It has four layers. The outer layer is the **crust**. It is solid rock. The rock is from 5 to 20 miles thick, and is thicker underneath the continents. The next layer is called the **mantle**. It is the thickest layer, about 1,800 miles thick and made up of rock. This rock may move because of the high temperatures and great pressure found there. The third layer is the **outer core**. It is liquid, or melted iron. This layer is about 1,400 miles thick. The innermost layer is the **inner core**. It is made of iron and nickel. It is extremely hot, reaching temperatures of more than 9,000°F. This is a solid mass of rock and is about 800 miles thick.

Directions: Label the layers of the earth. Then, answer the questions.

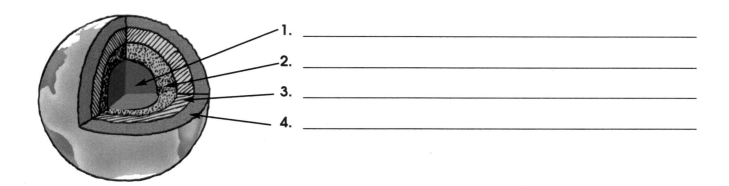

1. _____

2. _____

3. _____

4. _____

5. Which layer of the earth do you think shows the most evidence of an earthquake?

   _____

   _____

6. How do you think scientists find out about the inner cores of the earth?

   _____

   _____

Molten Rocks

There are three main classes of rocks. **Sedimentary** and **metamorphic** are two classes. The other class of rocks in the earth's crust formed from cooled lava, or **magma**. The lava came to the surface of earth, and the magma solidified.

Directions: To find out this last class of rocks, correctly fit the rocks listed below into the spaces. The circled letters will spell out the other class of rocks to which all of these rocks belong.

WORD BANK

basalt   diorite
feldspar   granite
obsidian   olivine
quartz

1. ___ ___ ___ ◯ ___ ___ ___ ___

2. ◯ ___ ___ ___ ___ ___ ___

3. ___ ___ ___ ___ ◯ ___ ___

4. ___ ◯ ___ ___ ___ ___ ___

5. ___ ◯ ___ ___ ___ ___ ___

6. ___ ◯ ___ ___ ___ ___

7. ___ ___ ◯ ___ ___ ___

8. Class of rocks: ___ ___ ___ ___ ___ ___ ___

9. Use a reference book to identify some of the major uses of these rocks.

_____

_____

_____

10. Where are these rocks found in the world?

_____

_____

_____

Volcanoes

A volcano is an opening in the earth's surface through which gases, lava, and ash erupt.

Directions: To learn more about volcanoes, complete the crossword puzzle below.

WORD BANK
caldera
cone
crater
dike
dormant
extinct
geyser
lava
magma
Mt. St. Helens
pumice
pyroclastics
ring of fire
shield
strato
tsunami
vent

ACROSS

2. A large crater formed by the collapse of an overlying volcanic cone

5. The range around the Pacific Ocean where volcanoes mainly occur

8. Fluid rock that pours from a volcano

9. A volcano that is not erupting and is not likely to erupt in the future

11. A composite volcano composed of alternating layers of lava and pyroclastic material

12. Type of volcano that has a broad profile, such as Mauna Loa and Mauna Kea

14. The volcano that erupted in the state of Washington in 1980

15. A large seismic sea wave caused by a volcanic eruption or earthquake

16. Groundwater which can be heated by volcanic activity and produces a hot-water fountain that spouts, such as Old Faithful

DOWN

1. An opening in the earth's surface through which gases and lava may escape

3. An inactive volcano which is likely to erupt in the future

4. Depression which can be caused by the collapse of a volcano

6. Various-sized particles ejected by a volcano

7. A body of molten rock injected into a fissure in the earth

10. A cinder _____ volcano is one that has a conical shape and is composed mostly of cinder-sized pyroclastics.

13. A light, glassy rock formed from a frothy lava

14. Molten rock inside the earth

Published by Frank Schaffer Publications. Copyright protected.

47

Science: Grade 5

All About Earthquakes

Name _____

An earthquake is the sudden shaking of the ground that occurs when masses of rock change positions below the earth's surface.

Directions: Learn more about earthquakes by reading the clues below. Locate the term in the magic square that matches each clue. Then, write the number of the clue in the space. By recording all of the correct numbers, you will have produced a magic square. When you add the numbers across, down, or diagonally, you should get the same answer. The four squares in each corner of the big square and the four squares in the center of the big square will also give you the same answer when added together.

fault _____	San Francisco _____	strike-slip fault _____	focus _____
normal fault _____	Richter scale _____	primary waves _____	Buffalo, NY _____
secondary waves _____	surface waves _____	oil and fossils _____	epicenter _____
reverse fault _____	San Andreas Fault _____	seismograph _____	seismologist _____

1. A fracture within the earth where rock movement occurs
2. An instrument used to measure earthquakes
3. A large fault in California
4. The point in the earth where seismic waves originate
5. The point on the earth's surface directly above the focus
6. A numerical scale used to express the strength of an earthquake
7. Seismic waves from the focus that are compressional
8. Seismic waves from the focus that are perpendicular to this motion
9. Location of the National Center for Earthquake Engineering Research
10. The most powerful shock waves from an earthquake
11. Sometimes located in the earth by seismic waves from explosions
12. Rock above a fault that moves downward
13. Rock above a fault that moves upward
14. Rocks that move in opposite horizontal directions
15. City which had major earthquakes in 1906 and 1989
16. Scientist who studies earthquakes

Atmospheric Circulation

Directions: There are five zones of atmospheric circulation on earth. To find out what they are, begin with the letter D on the spiral and skip every other letter to spell out these five zones. Write the names of the zones in the spaces at the bottom of the page.

The five zones are: __ __ __ __ __ __ __ __

__ __ __ __ __   __ __ __ __ __

__ __ __ __ __ __ __ __ __ __   __ __ __ __ __ __ __ __ __ __

__ __ __ __ __   __ __ __ __ __ __ __ __ __ __

__ __ __ __ __ __   __ __ __ __ __ __ __ __ __

Stormy Weather

Directions: Below is a list of stormy weather words. Locate and circle these words in the grid. The words may be written up, down, forward, backward, or diagonally. Then, look for a hidden word that is a type of storm. Draw a box around this word.

 WORD BANK

blizzard	cyclone	hail	hurricane
ice	lightning	monsoon	sandstorm
sleet	snow	squall	thunder
tornado	twister	waterspout	wind

```
D N A S M Q S M O L T E A R E
B A C M R O A T L E S L E E T
C L E G I D N H B F O N J L O
V L I A H P D U D S U W Y Q R
A H E Z T L S N O C F G I H N
D J L G Z L T D Q S U N P N A
N Y Z W K A O E A R W I X V D
I E G C H U R R I C A N E B O
W J L P N Q M D O K T T Q E R
H N R I U S X V W S E H W N T
M O Y E D A E O G D R G C O B
P O Z F T H N I K M S I N L J
R S V Q O S H E A R P L T C U
Z N X A D W I Z C G O B F Y E
J O L I N P R W K M U H E C I
Y M T S U D O Z T A T Y W U S
```

Write about an experience you have had in one of these storms.

_____

_____

_____

_____

_____

Name _____

Every three to seven years, the sea surface of the southeastern tropical Pacific warms to an unusually high temperature. Since ocean temperatures substantially affect the earth's weather, man and nature feel the effects of these El Niños. Historians suggest, in fact, that many flooding episodes and other weather events throughout history have been caused by El Niño's warming of ocean waters. What do you know about El Niños?

Directions: Place a **T** before each true statement and an **F** before each false statement.

_____ **1.** A Peruvian fisherman named the El Niño effect after the Christ Child because El Niños affect weather patterns from around Christmas until near Easter time.

_____ **2.** During the 1997-1998 El Niño, coastal flooding increased in California, Oregon, and Washington.

_____ **3.** El Niños increase easterly winds blowing across the tropical Pacific.

_____ **4.** El Niños commonly increase hurricane activity in the North Atlantic.

_____ **5.** The abnormal ocean temperature warming of an El Niño typically occurs during the months of December through March.

_____ **6.** During the 1997-1998 El Niño, southern Alaska experienced warmer and wetter conditions than normal.

_____ **7.** During a 1982–1983 El Niño, the French Polynesia suffered six major typhoons.

_____ **8.** The 1982-1983 hurricane season in the Atlantic experienced only two storms—the fewest it had experienced in a single season in 50 years.

_____ **9.** Weaker than normal trade winds alert meteorologists to a possible El Niño season.

_____ **10.** A 1972-1973 El Niño ruined fishing in Peru by turning the normally deep, cold, nutrient-rich waters of the western Pacific into warm, shallow waters that did not support anchovy life.

_____ **11.** Because expected monsoon rains fell before they reached the continent, the 1972-1973 El Niño caused a severe drought in India.

_____ **12.** Because the earth's weather patterns are not significantly tied together, El Niños do not affect the entire globe.

_____ **13.** During 1982 and 1983, eastern Australia, southern Africa, and Indonesia suffered severe droughts due to the effects of an El Niño.

_____ **14.** Fish that live in cold waters and birds that eat them usually survive the warm waters of an El Niño.

_____ **15.** The continent that suffers the most economic hardships from El Niño is South America.

_____ **16.** The most severe El Niño of the twentieth century occurred in 1997-1998.

Name

Human beings are not the only ones who can predict a rainstorm like the one that broke the South Fork Dam. Plants and animals sense atmospheric changes, too.

Directions: Match the following weather sayings with the reasons they often hold true. The first one has been done for you.

_B_ 1. Birds flying low, expect rain and a blow.

____2. If garden spiders forsake their webs, it indicates rain.

____3. Bees never get caught in the rain.

____4. If ants their walls do frequent build, Rain will from the clouds be spilled.

____5. The gnats bite and I scratch in vain Because they know it is going to rain.

____6. When leaves show their undersides Be very sure that rain betides.

____7. Seaweed dry, sunny sky. Seaweed wet, rain you'll get.

____8. Flowers smell best just before a rain.

____9. Knots get tighter before a rain.

___10. When the milkweed closes its pod, expect rain.

___11. Frogs croaking in the lagoon Means that rain will come real soon.

___12. Mushrooms and toadstools are plentiful before rain.

A. Ice crystals in clouds destroy the polarization of sunlight, making it difficult for bees to navigate, so they stay close to the hive in wet weather.

B. Low barometric pressure, which indicates precipitation, makes flying low in the sky easier than flying higher for birds.

C. Leaves curl and turn over on their branches before a rain.

D. Mushroom growth requires high humidity.

E. Insects fly lower and bite more in lowering pressure and rising humidity.

F. Plants sense moisture in the air and either close for protection or open to gather more rain water.

G. Water molecules help aromatic molecules bind better to the moisture in your nose.

H. When spider web threads absorb moisture, they break.

I. Ants reinforce their nests and cover their entrances before a rain.

J. Cold-blooded, aquatic animals require warm, moist conditions to be active.

K. Rope made of plant fibers expands when moisture fills its cellulose fibers.

L. Seaweed and moss absorb moisture.

Changing Faces

As the moon revolves around the earth, we can see different amounts of the moon's lighted part.

Directions: Study the drawing of the moon's different phases and each phase as it would be seen from the earth. Label each phase.

 WORD BANK

new moon	waxing crescent	first quarter
waxing gibbous	full moon	waning gibbous
last quarter	waning crescent	

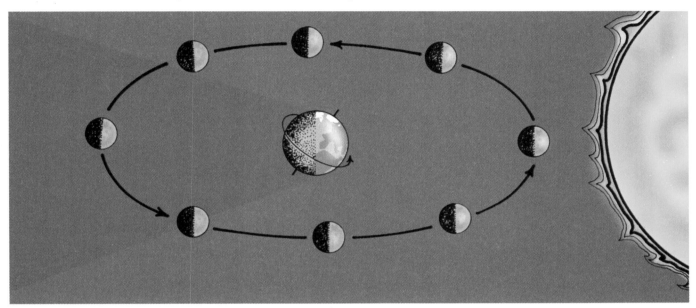

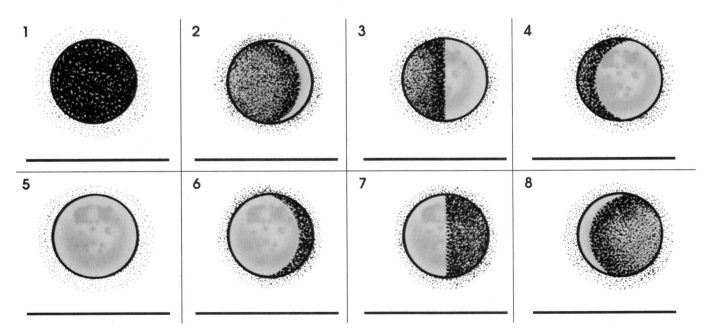

1 _____

2 _____

3 _____

4 _____

5 _____

6 _____

7 _____

8 _____

The ocean tides are caused mostly by the moon's gravity. When the sun, moon, and earth line up, the gravitational pull is greatest causing the highest tides, the spring tides. The lowest tides, neap tides, occur when the sun, earth, and moon form right angles.

Directions: Label the neap tides, spring tides, sun, earth, and moon.

WORD BANK

neap tides	spring tides	sun
moon	earth	

_____ tides

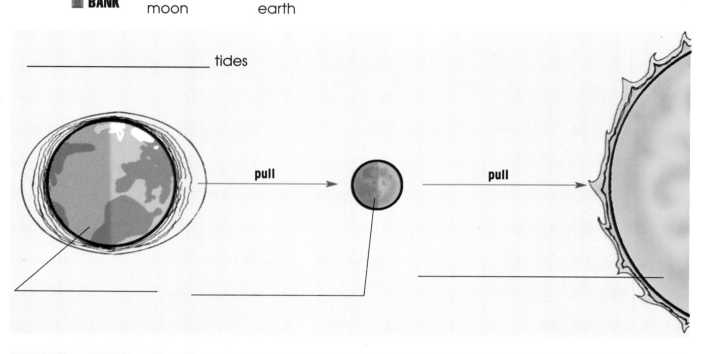

_____ tides

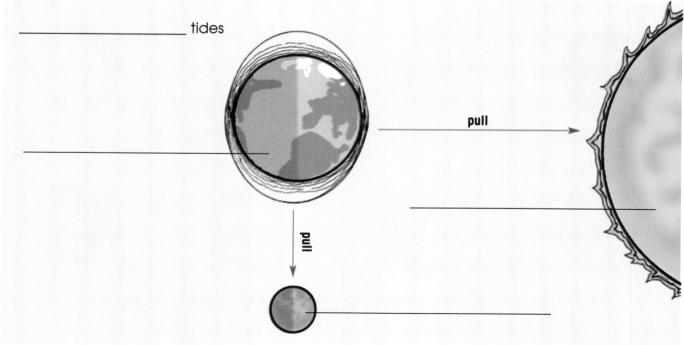

A Sunny Star

Looking out of the bus or car window, or looking around you as you walk to school, you can see the effects of the sun. It lights your way to school. It heats up the air around you. It helps plants grow and its energy even provides people with some needed vitamins.
The sun is a star. A star is really a ball of hot, glowing gases with no ground to stand on like the earth. Hydrogen is the main gas in the sun. It is the hydrogen that provides the energy the sun needs to make the light and heat for the earth, which is millions of miles away.

The sun is the star in the center of the solar system. All planets revolve around the sun. It is average in size for a star, with a diameter of about 863,710 mi. The sun is almost half way through its life, which is about 9 billion years long.

Directions: Answer the following questions using the information above.

1. What is a star?

   _____

   _____

2. What is the diameter of the sun? How does it compare to the size of other stars?

   _____

   _____

3. We know the earth revolves around the sun. What happens on the earth as a result of that revolving?

   _____

   _____

4. What might it be like on the earth if the sun were to burn out?

   _____

   _____

   _____

Name _____

Directions: The sun is the closest star to the earth. Use the WORD BANK to label the different layers and features of the sun.

 WORD BANK

core   radiative zone   sunspot
photosphere   chromosphere   flare
prominence

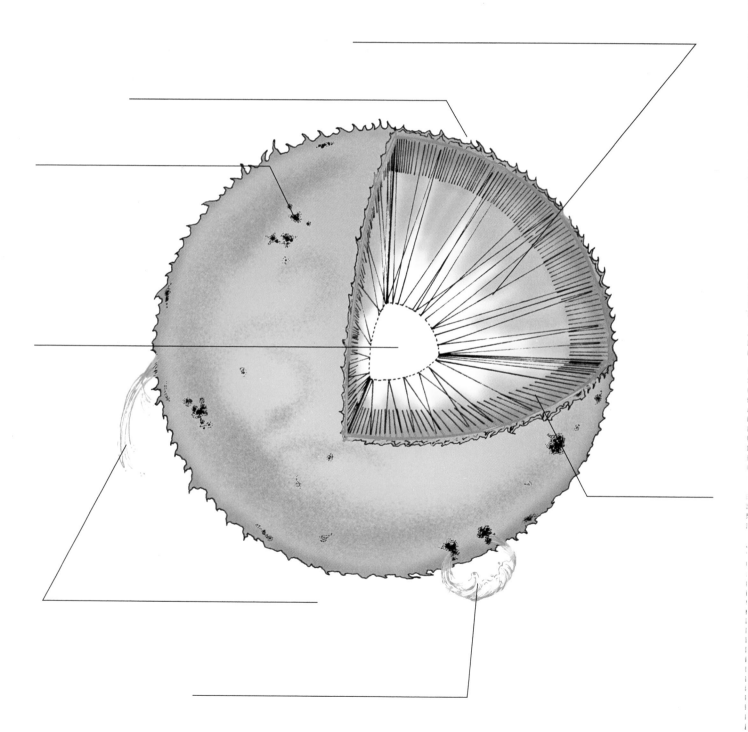

Name

The diagram below shows the earth's position in its orbit on four different dates.

Directions: On the solid line label the equinox dates. On the dotted lines name the season for the Northern Hemisphere.

 WORD BANK

| March 21 | December 22 | spring | fall |
| September 22 | June 21 | winter | summer |

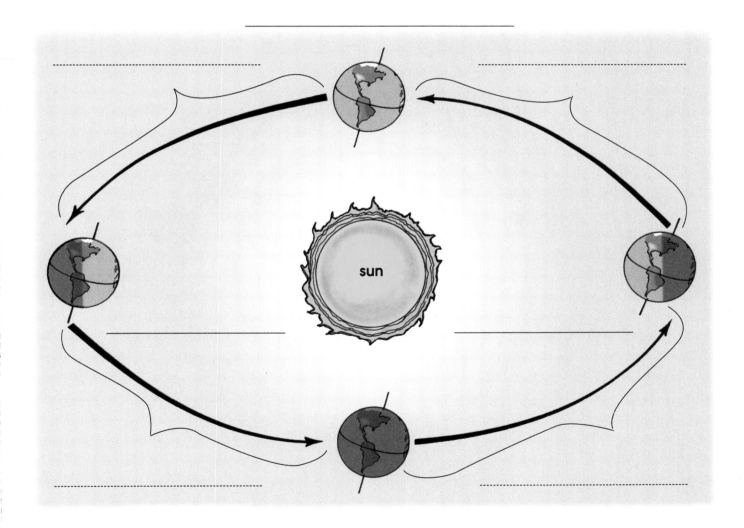

Directions: All of the planets of the solar system travel around the sun. Label the planets.

WORD BANK

Mercury	Venus	Earth
Mars	Jupiter	Saturn
Uranus	Neptune	Pluto

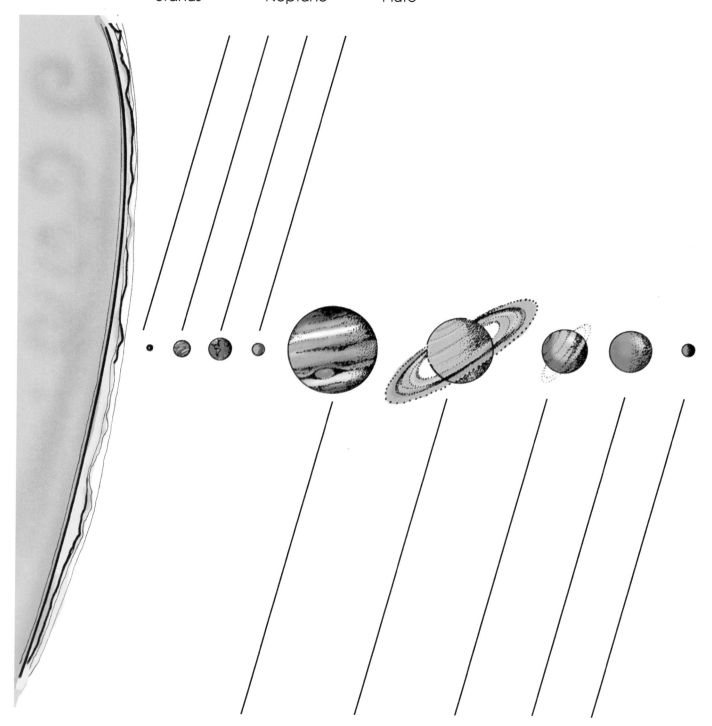

Astronomers have divided the sky into 88 constellations. The letters in the blocks below will spell out the names of 12 constellations found in the sky. The beginning letter of each constellation is in the star.

Directions: Draw straight lines between the letters to find the name of each constellation. No lines will cross. Write the name of each constellation at the bottom of the page.

1. T T A R I U S ☆S I G A

2. U Q R A ☆A U I S

3. E ☆G M I N I

4. ☆C I A C P R O U S N

5. O C R O ☆S I P

6. E ☆P C S I S

7. S A ☆T U U R

8. ☆C E C N R A

9. O ☆V G I R

10. ☆L I B A R

11. ☆A R E S I

12. ☆L E O

1. _____

2. _____

3. _____

4. _____

5. _____

6. _____

7. _____

8. _____

9. _____

10. _____

11. _____

12. _____

Hello Out There!

Our earth and sun belong to a vast number of stars called the Milky Way Galaxy. The word galaxy comes from a Greek word meaning "milk."

Directions: Use the code below to design a message you would send to outer space to tell any possible life forms in the Milky Way about earth.

Letter	Pattern (top / mid / bottom)		Letter	Pattern (top / mid / bottom)
A	●○ / ○○ / ○○		N	●○ / ○● / ○○
B	○○ / ●○ / ○○		O	●○ / ○● / ○●
C	○○ / ○○ / ●○		P	○● / ●○ / ○○
D	○● / ○○ / ○○		Q	○○ / ●○ / ○●
E	○○ / ○● / ○○		R	○● / ○○ / ●○
F	○○ / ○○ / ○●		S	○○ / ○● / ●○
G	●○ / ●○ / ○○		T	●● / ●○ / ○○
H	○○ / ●○ / ●○		U	○● / ●○ / ○○
I	○● / ○● / ○○		V	●● / ○● / ○○
J	○○ / ○● / ○●		W	●○ / ○● / ○●
K	●● / ○● / ○○		X	●○ / ○● / ●○
L	○○ / ●● / ○○		Y	○● / ○● / ○●
M	○○ / ○○ / ●●		Z	●● / ●● / ●●

1. Decode the message.

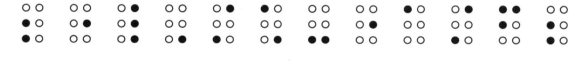

___ ___ ___ ___ ___ ___ ___ ___ ___ ___ ___ ___

2. Design your own message to send. Exchange it with a friend to decode.

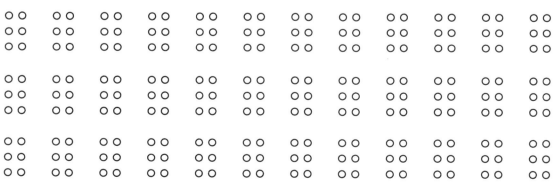

60 *Science: Grade 5*

Name _____

Beyond our galaxy lie billions of other galaxies.

Directions: Use the WORD BANK to label the shapes of some of these galaxies.

WORD BANK   elliptical   spiral   barred spiral   irregular

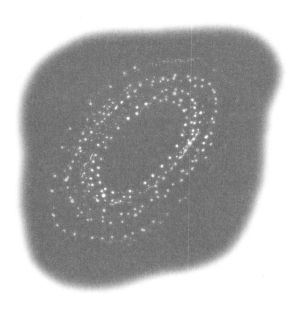

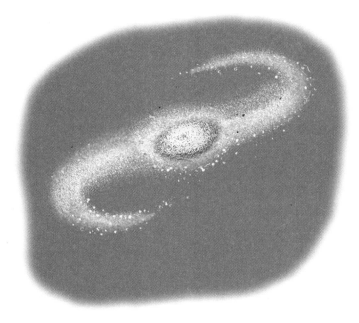

_____   _____

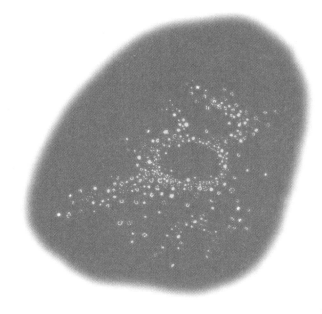

_____   _____

Name _____

Directions: Label the parts of the helium atom pictured below.

WORD BANK   proton   nucleus   neutron
                orbit (shell) electron

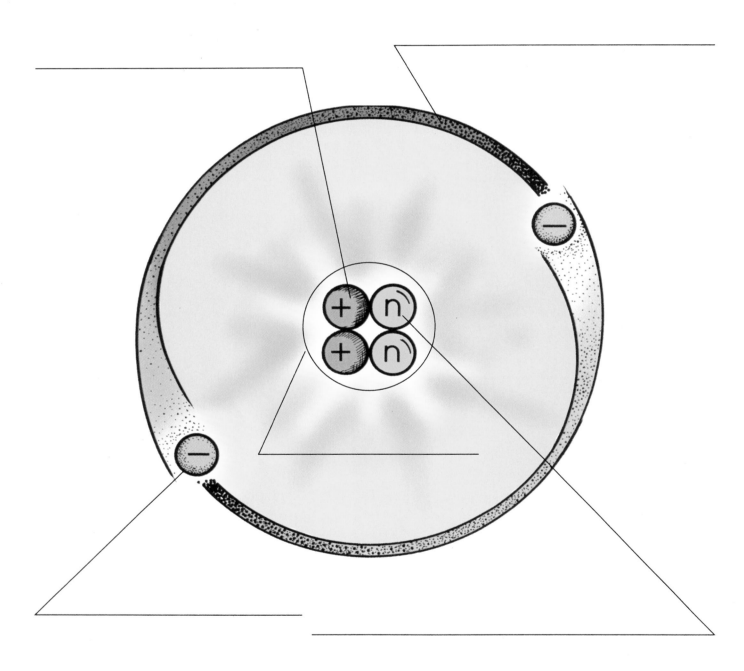

Matter is anything that has mass and takes up space. Everything is matter. We can classify all of the matter in the world into one of three groups: elements, compounds, and mixtures.

An **element** is matter that is made up of only one ingredient. Oxygen, hydrogen, and carbon are elements. We can find the names of the different elements that make up our world on a special table known as the Periodic Table. Most of the elements on this table are made by nature. The other elements are made by scientists. Elements are just one type of matter, but without them, compounds and mixtures could not exist.

A **compound** is matter that is made up of two or more ingredients that are joined together. The ingredients cannot be taken apart easily. Water, sugar, a piece of cake, a fork, and the wood on a cabinet drawer are compounds. Most of the matter in our world exists as a compound.

A **mixture** is matter that is made up of two or more ingredients that are mixed together. The ingredients in a mixture are easy to take apart. Cereal in milk, trail mix, and Italian salad dressing are mixtures.

Matter has observable properties. A property is a characteristic we can use to identify something. We make observations using our senses and measurements. Observable properties include color, texture, size, weight, taste, smell, and sound. The color and texture of a chocolate chip cookie allow us to identify it from a sugar cookie.

Directions: Answer the questions using the information in the reading.

1. What is matter? _____

2. What are the three different types of matter? _____

_____

3. How are the three types of matter alike? _____

_____

4. How are the three types of matter different? _____

_____

5. What is a property? _____

_____

6. Name at least four different properties that can be used to identify you.

_____

A Chemical Change

One way that matter changes is chemically. A chemical change, also called a **chemical reaction**, actually changes the matter from the original form to something else. This type of change involves giving off or taking in energy. The energy that helps the change happen may be in several different forms, such as electricity or heat. Sometimes the change occurs so slowly, we hardly notice.

One example of chemical change that we can observe in the lunchroom is fresh baked cookies resulting from the heating of cookie dough. Another is old, brown apple slices on a dish.

Directions: On the line write **Chemical** if it is a chemical change or **Physical** if it is a physical change.

_____ **1.** Tarnish on silver

_____ **2.** Bread baking in the oven

_____ **3.** Cutting paper hearts from red paper

_____ **4.** Mixing sugar into water

_____ **5.** Burning toast in the toaster

_____ **6.** Rust forming on a tin can

Name _____

Directions: Anything that contains space is considered to be matter. Matter can be a solid, a liquid, or a gas. Read the definitions below. Use the words in the box to fill in the blanks after each definition. Then, write the circled letters in order to spell out the names of a person who studies the changes in the states of matter.

WORD BANK

boiling	freezing	solidification
condensation	liquefaction	sublimation
evaporation	melting	vaporization

1. Molten lava changes into solid rock. ◯__ __ __ __ __ __ __ __ __ __ __ __

2. Dew forms on the grass. ◯__ __ __ __ __ __ __ __ __ __ __

3. Hot lava flows into the ocean and quickly changes water into water vapor. __ __ __ __ __◯__ __ __ __ __

4. Solid ice changes to a liquid. __◯__ __ __ __ __

5. Water reaches 212 degrees Fahrenheit. __ __ __ __ __◯__

6. Water in a vase changes to water vapor. __ __ __ __ __ __ __◯__ __ __

7. Water reaches 32 degrees Fahrenheit. __ __ __ __ __◯__ __

8. Dry ice changes from a solid to a gas. ◯__ __ __ __ __ __ __ __ __ __

9. Oxygen in the air is cooled until it becomes a liquid. __ __ __ __ __ __ __ __◯__ __ __

Person: __ __ __ __ __ __ __ __ __ .

Physical and Chemical Changes

Name _____

Objects undergo many kinds of changes. Place a **P** in front of each physical change below and a **C** in front of each chemical change.

_____ 1. Rusting of iron

_____ 2. Breaking of a tree limb

_____ 3. Cutting paper

_____ 4. Action of yeast in breadmaking

_____ 5. Souring of milk

_____ 6. Wadding up a sheet of paper

_____ 7. Erasing a pencil mark

_____ 8. Freezing of water

_____ 9. Boiling water

_____ 10. Salting the ice on a sidewalk

_____ 11. Action of baking powder in cooking a cake

_____ 12. Bending a metal wire

_____ 13. Etching glass with acid

_____ 14. Formation of stalagmites in a cave

_____ 15. Fertilizing a lawn

_____ 16. Crushing ice in a blender

_____ 17. Evaporation of water in a lake

_____ 18. Eating foods

_____ 19. Burning gasoline in a car engine

_____ 20. Burning logs in a fireplace

_____ 21. Toasting marshmallows over a campfire

_____ 22. Adding bleach to a washer of clothes

_____ 23. Slicing a block of cheese

Three Classes of Levers

There are three classes of levers—first-class, second-class, and third-class. All levers have a resistance arm, an effort arm, and a fulcrum. Examine the sketches of the three classes of levers below for the positions of the fulcrum, the effort arm, and the resistance arm.

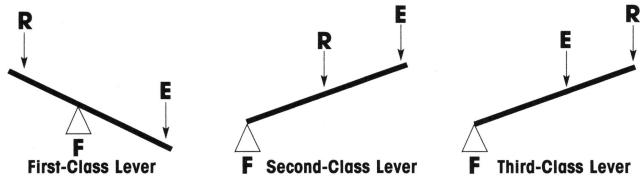

| First-Class Lever | Second-Class Lever | Third-Class Lever |

Directions: Make a simple sketch of the events below. Label the fulcrum, the effort arm, and the resistance arm. Identify the class of lever.

1. Two students on a seesaw	**2.** Using a nutcracker
3. Sweeping with a broom	**4.** Using a car jack
5. Rolling a wheelbarrow	**6.** Batting a baseball
7. Hammering a nail in a board	**8.** Swinging a golf club

There are six simple machines that are the basic units of all complex machines: the **lever**, the **wheel and axle**, the **wedge**, the **pulley**, the **inclined plane**, and the **screw**.

RECOGNIZING SIMPLE MACHINES

Which simple machines can you find in each of the tools listed below?

hammer _____   scissors _____

doorstop _____   drill _____

saw _____   screwdriver _____

crowbar _____   monkey wrench _____

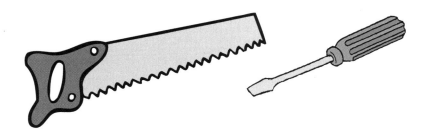

BICYCLE PARTS

Study a bicycle carefully. Fill in the blanks with the simple machines you find.

tire _____   kickstand _____

caliper brakes _____   handlebars _____

chain and sprocket _____   gearshift _____

pedal and shaft _____   fork _____

other _____

_____

Compound Machines

Often two or more simple machines are combined to make one machine called a **compound machine**.

Directions: Name the simple machines that are combined to make each of the compound machines pictured below.

WORD BANK   wheel and axle   inclined plane (wedge, screw)
                lever   pulley

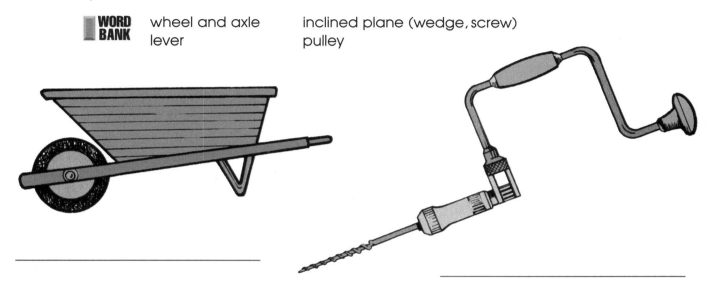

_____

_____

_____

Page 3
Sort 'Em Out

VERTEBRATES		INVERTEBRATES
1.	dog	1. octopus
2.	boy	2. snail
3.	turtle	3. starfish
4.	frog	4. lobster
5.	lizard	5. oyster

Page 4
Classifying Vertebrates

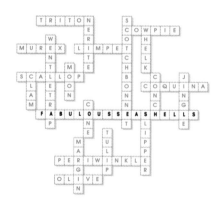

	FISH	AMPHIBIANS	BIRDS	REPTILES	MAMMALS
Body covering	scales	smooth	feathers	scales or shell	hair or fur
Warm- or cold-blooded	cold	cold	warm	cold	warm
Lungs or gills	gills	gills/lungs	lungs	lungs	lungs
Born alive or hatched	both	hatched	hatched	both	born
Habitat	water	water/land	air and water	water/land	land, air, and water
Name one example	Answers will vary.				

Page 5
Have You Seen It?
A. wings—thorax
B. antennae—head
C. eyes—head
D. spiracles—abdomen
E. legs—thorax
F. mouth—head

Page 6
All Kinds of Reptiles

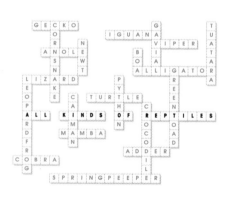

Page 7
Fabulous Seashells

Page 8
Hide-and-Seek
1. Animal choices will vary.
2. Camouflage can hide animals from predators and help them sneak up on their prey.
3. Answers may include color and texture.

Page 9
Your Body Parts

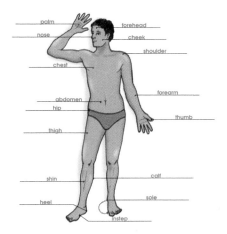

Page 10
Skeletal System Review

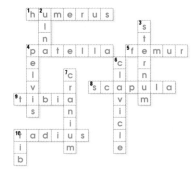

Page 11
Muscle Man

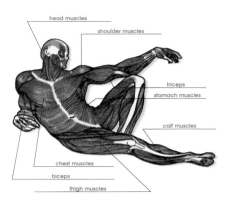

Page 12
The Circulatory System I
1. transporting materials throughout the body and regulating body temperature
2. cells
3. waste products; liver, lungs, kidneys
4. center, surface
5. Blood vessels contract, allowing little blood to flow through.
A "Hearty" Experiment:
Answers will vary.

Page 13
The Circulatory System II

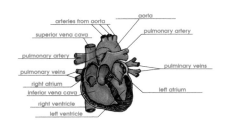

Page 14
Circulatory System Review

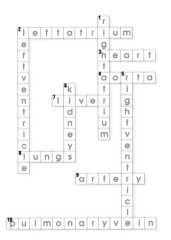

Page 15
The Respiratory System

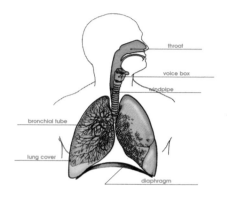

Page 16
Respiratory System Review

Page 17
Your Digestive System

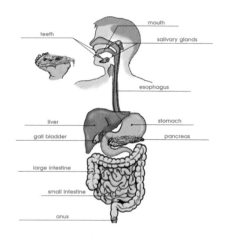

Page 18
The Alimentary Canal

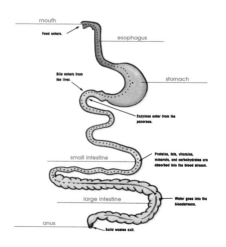

Page 19
Digestive System Review

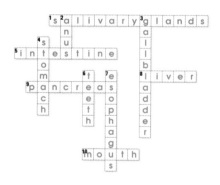

Page 20
Waste Removal

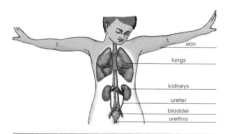

FUNCTION	EXCRETORY ORGANS			
	Kidneys	Lungs	Skin	Bladder
Removes water	✓	✓	✓	
Brings oxygen to blood		✓		
Removes salt	✓		✓	
Stores urine				✓
Removes carbon dioxide		✓		
Produces urine	✓			
Removes body heat		✓	✓	

Answer Key

Page 21
Blood Scrubbers

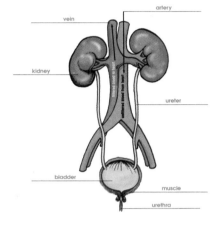

Page 23
The Central Nervous System

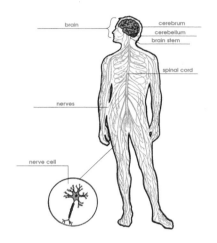

Page 24
The Endocrine System

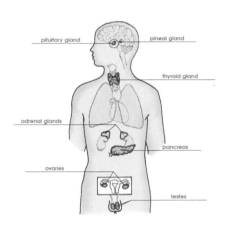

Page 25
Skin Deep

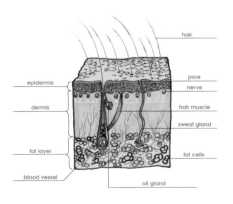

Page 26
Body Tissues

connective tissue

muscle tissue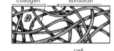

nerve tissue

epithelial tissue

Page 27
A Special Science Tool
a. nosepiece
b. coarse adjustment
c. fine adjustment
d. arm
e. base
f. eyepiece
g. body tube
h. objective
i. stage
j. diaphragm
k. stage clips
l. mirror

Answer Key

Page 28
Photosynthesis

Page 29
Root Systems

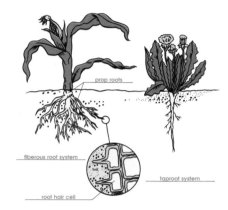

Page 30
Inside a Root

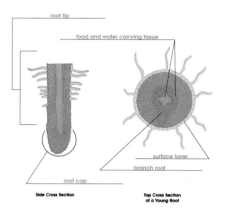

Page 31
A Seedy Start
1. warmth, air, and water
2. through seeds
3. the seed coat, the embryo, the food supply
4. it sprouts
5. the roots

Page 32
Sailing Seeds
1. man plants seeds
2. seeds travel in water
3. seeds stick to leg
4. seeds travel by wind
5. birds carry seeds

Page 33
Making Seeds
1. petal—red
2. sepal—green
3. stamen—brown
4. pistil—yellow
5. ovary—blue

Page 34
All About Growing

Page 35
Which Is It?
1. **a.** producer
   b. herbivore
   c. carnivore
2. **a.** producer
   b. herbivore
   c. omnivore
3. **a.** producer
   b. herbivore
   c. carnivore

Page 36
What We Need
Fruit—1
Milk—2, 8, 12
Fats and Sweets—3, 11
Vegetables—4, 9
Meat—5, 10
Grains—6, 7

Page 37
Where's the Energy?
1. the amount of energy supplied by carbohydrates, proteins, and fats as they are digested
2. proteins, carbohydrates, and fats
3. carbohydrates and proteins; eating too many fats is unhealthy
4. you gain weight

Page 38
Reading the Label
1. 2 teas. every 6 hours
2. 1 teas. every 6 hours
3. drowsiness
4. child under 5; pregnant or nursing mother
5. 4
6. August 1993
7. Consult your physician.
8. coughs due to colds and flu

Page 39
Life on a Rotting Log
1. lichen, moss, mushrooms
2. The roots create open spaces in the log.
3. The log offers plants a source of food, protection, and a place to grow
4. salamander, ants, earthworms, chipmunk
5. They eat and chew on the log. A lichen is made up of an algae and a fungus. The algae makes food by means of photosynthesis. The fungus absorbs the water that the algae needs to live

Page 40
Mineral Identifications

MINERAL	HARDNESS	SPECIFIC GRAVITY	STREAK COLOR	LUSTER
Siderite	3.5–4	3.85	white	pearly
Gypsum	2	2.32	white	vitreous
Kaolinite	2–2.5	2.6	white	dull
Halite	2.5	2.16	white	glassy
Fluorite	4	3–3.3	white	glassy
Calcite	3	2.7	white	waxy
Barite	3–3.5	4.3–4.6	white	vitreous
Pyrite	6–6.5	5.02	green-black	metallic
Galena	2.5–2.7	7.4–7.6	lead-gray	metallic
Magnetite	6	5.2	black	metallic
Topaz	8	3.4–3.6	colorless	glassy

1. gypsum, kaolinite, halite
2. gypsum, kaolinite, halite, calcite, galena
3. pyrite, magnetite, topaz
4. topaz

Page 41
Name That Mineral

The Unknown Minerals

HARDNESS	COLOR	LUSTER	MINERAL
Will scratch a steel knife or window glass.	yellow	glassy	Quartz
Will scratch a steel knife or window glass.	gray	glassy	Feldspar
A copper penny will scratch it	black	pearly	Mica
Fingernail will scratch it.	white	pearly	Talc
Knife blade or window glass will scratch it.	black	glassy	Hornblende

Page 42
Classy Rocks
igneous
metamorphic
metamorphic
sedimentary
sedimentary
igneous
sedimentary
metamorphic
igneous
sedimentary
cooled magma
layers of loose material, etc.
rock that has been changed, etc

Page 43
Rocks and Minerals

Page 44
Glaciers
1. B
2. G
3. J
4. C
5. L
6. K
7. N
8. I
9. M
10. E
11. F
12. D
13. H
14. A

Page 45
The Layered Look
1. inner core
2. outer core
3. mantle
4. crust
5. crust
6. Answers will vary.

Answer Key

Page 46
Molten Rocks
1. obsidian
2. granite
3. olivine
4. feldspar
5. diorite
6. quartz
7. basalt
8. igneous
9. buildings, statues, cutting tools, decorative objects, sand, glass, electronic equipment
10. western U.S., Mexico, Hawaii, Italy, South Africa, Canada, North Carolina, Georgia

Page 47
Volcanoes

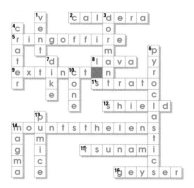

Page 48
All About Earthquakes

fault	San Francisco	strike-slip fault	focus
1	15	14	4
normal fault	Richter scale	primary waves	Buffalo, NY
12	6	7	9
secondary waves	surface waves	oil and fossils	epicenter
8	10	11	5
reverse fault	San Andreas Fault	seismograph	seismologist
13	3	2	16

Page 49
Atmospheric Circulation
doldrums, trade winds, prevailing easterlies, prevailing westerlies, horse latitudes

Page 50
Stormy Weather

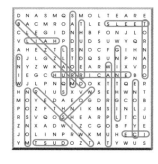

Page 51
The Effects of El Niño
1. T
2. T
3. F—El Niños slow easterly winds across the tropical Pacific to an almost standstill.
4. F—The El Niño effect increases hurricane activity in the North Pacific, but it decreases it in the North Atlantic.
5. T
6. F—Alaska experienced warmer and drier weather than normal that season.
7. T—Incidentally, the region is accustomed to only one typhoon every three years.
8. T
9. F—Stronger than normal trade winds predict El Niños.
10. T
11. T
12. F—El Niños can affect the entire globe.
13. T
14. F—Fish and birds die or leave the region during El Niños.
15. T
16. F—The most severe El Niño of the twentieth century occurred in 1982-1983

Page 52
Natural Weather Forecasters
1. B
2. H
3. A
4. I
5. E
6. C
7. L
8. G
9. K
10. F
11. J
12. D

Page 53
Changing Faces

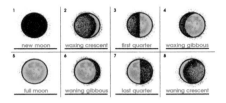

Page 54
High Tide

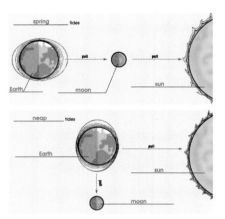

Page 55
A Sunny Star
1. ball of hot, glowing gases with no ground
2. 863,710 miles in diameter. It is average in size.
3. four seasons
4. Life as we know it would stop.

Page 56
Our Closest Star—the Sun

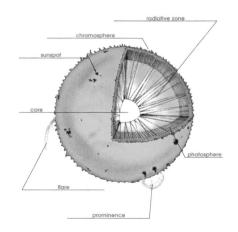

Page 57
The Seasons

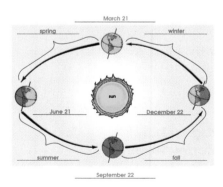

Page 58
Planets of the Solar System

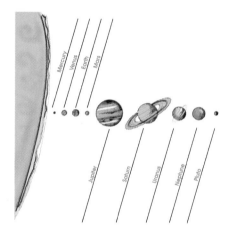

Page 59
Constellations of the Zodiac
1. Sagittarius
2. Aquarius
3. Gemini
4. Capricornus
5. Scorpio
6. Pisces
7. Taurus
8. Cancer
9. Virgo
10. Libra
11. Aries
12. Leo

Page 60
Hello Out There!
1. Hey from Earth
2. Messages will vary.

Page 61
Galaxies
elliptical
barred spiral
spiral
irregular

Page 62
Atoms

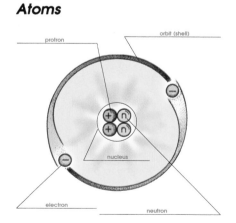

Page 63
What's the Matter?
1. anything that has mass and takes up space
2. elements, compounds, and mixtures
3. Answers will vary.
4. Answers will vary.
5. an observable characteristic that can be used to identify something
6. Answers will vary.

Page 64
A Chemical Change
1. chemical
2. chemical
3. physical
4. physical
5. chemical
6. chemical

Page 65
Changes in the States of Matter
1. solidification
2. condensation
3. vaporization
4. melting
5. boiling
6. evaporation
7. freezing
8. sublimation
9. liquefaction

scientist

Page 66
Physical and Chemical Changes
1. C
2. P
3. P
4. C
5. C
6. P
7. P
8. P
9. P
10. C
11. C
12. P
13. C
14. C
15. C
16. P
17. P
18. C
19. C
20. C
21. C
22. C
23. P

Page 67
Three Classes of Levers
1. first
2. second
3. third
4. first
5. second
6. third
7. third
8. third

Page 68
Simple Machines

hammer	lever	scissors	levers
doorstop	wedge	drill	screw
saw	wedge	screwdriver	wheel and axle
crowbar	lever	monkey wrench	wheel and axle

BICYCLE PARTS
Study a bicycle carefully. Fill in the blanks with the simple machines you find.

tire	wheel and axle	kickstand	inclined plane
caliper brakes	lever	handlebars	lever
chain and sprocket	pulley	gearshift	wheel and axle
pedal and shaft	wheel and axle	fork	lever
other			

Page 69
Compound Machines

lever, wheel and axle

screw, wheel and axle

pulley, wheel and axle, lever